LETTING GO ; LOVING FOREVER

LETTING GO ; LOVING FOREVER

MARGARET & LILO BAURER

Letting Go; Loving Forever **by Margaret & Lilo Baurer**

9 8 7 6 5 4 3 2 1

First Edition

Printed in the United States of America.

Project managers: Deanna Novak and Brian Walls, Pithy Wordsmithery

Cover design by James and Jon Sholly, Pithy Wordsmithery

Interior layout by Sue Murray, Pithy Wordsmithery

Copyediting by Nils Kuehn, Pithy Wordsmithery

Proofreading by Katharine Dvorak and Scott Morrow, Pithy Wordsmithery

ISBN: 979-8-9886185-0-8 (paperback)

ISBN: 979-8-9886185-1-5 (ebook)

ISBN: 979-8-9886185-2-2 (hardcover)

To contact the authors: hello@hopewardhealing.com, www.hopewardhealing.com

Library of Congress Control Number: 2023914577

Disclaimer
This work is a memoir and depicts actual events in the life of the author and her family, recounted over a period of time. They are presented as truthfully as recollection permits and/or can be verified by additional research. Occasionally, dialogue consistent with the character and nature of the person speaking has been supplemented. All persons within this book are actual individuals, there are no composite characters. The names of some individuals, institutions, outpatient programs, and residential treatment centers, however, have been changed to respect their privacy. The recounting of some events may be compressed and summarized for brevity's sake.

To my guardian angel, Jeff, and to our three stars, who continue to be the reason I get out of bed every morning.

—Margaret

To my dad, for being my inspiration as a creator and for being my anchor throughout my mental health journey.

—Lilo

TABLE OF CONTENTS

FOREWORD

Dear Reader,

You are about to meet and read a story about a family who will touch your life. I know this because I have been privileged to be a part of their story. As a clinical social worker specializing in thanatology (death, dying, and bereavement) for more than thirty years, I have walked with many people on their journeys. I think clients often do not realize how much they impact a therapist and how much we learn and change because of our interactions with them. I distinctly remember the day in November 2013 when Margaret and Lilo Baurer walked into my office seeking grief support for Lilo. Lilo was just eleven years old. This meeting launched a relationship with their family that would span years, challenge my skills as a therapist, inform my practice, and deeply enrich my life.

This first meeting occurred less than a year after Jeff Baurer, Margaret's spouse and father of Sarah (aged fifteen), Lilo, and Brooke (aged nine), died suddenly from a brain aneurysm at age forty-four. Family life instantly changed as they learned to cope with the pain of his absence and adjusted to altered household norms and routines. During that time, Lilo was navigating the difficulties of middle school and asked for help processing their grief. In session, Lilo was shy and tentative but also very engaging and creative. I observed Margaret, deep in her grief, fiercely devoted to the well-being of her family.

Grieving is a natural response to loss, and Lilo deeply missed their father. I was often amazed at their ability to express these emotions through art and poetry. As therapy evolved, I learned Lilo's grief was impacted by their adoption story, attachment ruptures, and a growing sense of depression and fragmentation. Our therapy work together became intense. Lilo's world became darker, and Margaret's fear for Lilo's safety became all-consuming. Lilo's admission of self-injury and suicidal ideation confirmed Margaret's worst fears. Margaret recalls the pit in her stomach when I would share with her, "Lilo cannot be left alone tonight." I remember my fear and worry for both of them as Lilo began withdrawing into their own world. We had reached a "tipping point," necessitating increased mental health services and treatment placements for Lilo to ensure their safety.

Lilo and Margaret write their story in powerful words in a narrative that is authentic and courageous. It is sometimes uncomfortable to read, just as it was painful to witness. Their experiences highlight the abyss of psychological pain and the underbelly of the mental health system; treatment limitations; the maze of diagnoses; insurance roadblocks; the financial cost; and the overarching dilemma of effectively coordinating treatment, school, and home life. I was allowed to be and accepted the importance of being a constant through the chaos, and I carefully made myself available to them. My role as therapist and case manager expanded to crisis intervention, resource collaborator, support person, and provider of psychoeducation when appropriate. I often shared the fear or anguish that Margaret experienced through validation and my own voice. The intensity of this story's events required us to be authentic, real, and present.

As I reflect on these years, I recognize that Lilo encouraged me to look outside the lines and to look at things differently from the day we met. Their experiences resonated with me, and their creativity literally left me in awe. I have witnessed Margaret's deep grief, the gripping terror of worry about her child's life, and the exhaustion of her interactions with systems. Yet, despite all of this, she demonstrated tenacity and willingness to change. I believe there were times all of us wondered where this would end. There have been tears, confrontations, anger, and disappointments—but also laughter, memories, and growth.

I believe we all have a story to tell. We write our own narratives, and sharing those stories makes a difference in others' lives. We often place ourselves in those stories and think about how we would have done things differently, questioning our decisions, reactions, or even the emotions we expressed.

I am confident you will be moved by the courage in their honest and transparent account, which shares two very different perspectives. I hope it also makes you think and question as issues of grief, mental health, and gender identity are explored. I hope their story helps you to value yours. I also hope you will be inspired by the thriving of others through their adversity and pain. Allow Margaret and Lilo's story to move you and encourage you to write your story in the way you wish. Lilo and Margaret changed me, both personally and as a therapist. I will be forever grateful to know them and to have traveled with them during these years.

Priscilla Brinkman, LCSW, FT

Postscript
I am humbled and feel a great responsibility to write this foreword. As a clinical social worker, I value and adhere to the strict confidential code of my professional ethics. The authors' request and permission to share my thoughts publicly is a true reflection of the time we have shared together.

INTRODUCTION

Life is filled with moments that permanently alter our path. After my husband's sudden and unexpected death, my child experienced serious and life-threatening mental health struggles, including several suicide attempts. Hearing about our difficult journey, many friends, and even a few acquaintances, suggested I write a book about our experience. After all, truth is often stranger than fiction. I never took their suggestions seriously. I was told our story sounded like the plot of a Lifetime movie. However, each time people suggested I put pen to paper, I brushed it off, just as I do when my children beg me to purchase a five-bedroom vacation home in Hawaii!

When my child came to me and asked if I would cowrite our story, I finally took the idea of writing a book to heart. Our story is extraordinarily complex and consists of many layers—*family, grief, mental health, gender identity,* and *the difficult road to finding acceptance.* This story is about my relationship with my child, Lilo. Despite the challenges of mental health diagnoses, changing gender identity, and experiencing great loss together, we set aside our differences to create a loving relationship. But the path to our now trusting and accepting relationship was difficult and riddled with obstacles. This story is a roller-coaster ride of unexpected twists and turns, steep slopes, and gut-wrenching plunges. It is also a story of love, loss, and acceptance.

My coauthor is not only my child but also the greatest teacher in my life. The lessons I have learned from Lilo are far too numerous to list here, but as you dive into the pages of this book, you will read about them. One of the greatest of these lessons was also the most difficult: *acceptance*. Our lives were chaotic, filled with sudden and unexpected turmoil, and often very dramatic. In the face of significant change, it was difficult for me to accept the new reality I was experiencing, especially as Lilo's identity began to change late into their teenage years.

When my middle child approached me to ask to be called Lilo instead of their given name, admittedly, I was scared and confused. It sounds like such a simple request that any loving mother would be happy to honor for her child. However, it was loaded with emotional baggage for me because of the memory of my late husband.

I married my best friend from childhood, and we became the parents of three beautiful daughters. Having three girls became part of our identities as parents. When our third daughter was born, we received greeting cards that welcomed us to the "three-girls club." When my husband passed away, our happily ever after was abruptly cut short. Jeff died proudly believing he was a three-girl dad.

Lilo may be a gender-neutral name, but it was also Jeff's nickname for our child. After his death, I considered his nickname almost sacred. At first, I was uncomfortable hearing Lilo's friends use this name for our child. It reminded me that Jeff was no longer with us to watch them mature into the fantastic young person they have become. It wasn't long before Lilo preferred gender-neutral pronouns too. As a worried mother, it was difficult navigating these turbulent changes. These changes in gender identity were heightened by the fact that much of their teenage years were spent in residential treatment facilities where I could not witness this shift in identity firsthand.

In the wake of these changes, I was consumed by loss. I had lost my role as Jeff's wife to his untimely death. I'd lost my child's given name when they legally changed it. So who was I if I was no longer a three-girl mom?

While Lilo was finding their true identity, I felt I was losing mine. It took a lot of self-work, therapy, and honest conversations to reach a place of acceptance. Accepting Lilo as transgender nonbinary somehow meant I was losing the part of Jeff that took such pride in his three daughters. It wasn't until I let go of my intense feelings of loss that I began to see what I was gaining: the incredible spirit of a kind, gentle, and inquisitive person named "Lilo." I explain the backstory behind Lilo's name (and my acceptance of who they are) because this book uses Lilo's preferred pronouns (they/them). I want to be honest and transparent when admitting that my acceptance of this change did not happen overnight. I don't want to mislead those parents going through similar situations. I can say that I do not wish Lilo to be anyone other than who they are and always have been.

Lilo is confident, creative, and one of the most genuine young adults I have ever known. They are also one of the most patient. I am incredibly proud to be Lilo's mother. Writing our story has been emotional yet tremendously cathartic. I laughed along the way, and I also cried on many occasions. It has been the privilege of a lifetime to write this book alongside Lilo.

As you read, you'll notice that this story is told by both of us in the way we each experienced it. Although the names of people and treatment facilities are changed for privacy, the exact same events are told from two vastly different perspectives. My hope is that this book can be an encouragement to families who are themselves traversing difficult experiences together. You don't always have to see eye to eye; this book is the culmination of that reality. It is a reminder that everyone's experience is different. No matter how difficult, the willingness to be vulnerable and share your story can be a profound gift to help others avoid your mistakes. We hope you find our story as inspiring as it is authentic. Most of all, we yearn to bring hope to those who are currently struggling so that they too may find the light through the darkness.

—Margaret

Chapter 1

MARGARET

I am not sure there is a little girl anywhere who, at some point during her childhood, did not dream of becoming a bride. I definitely remember standing in the kitchen and placing one of my mother's white tea towels on top of my head. All the movies and fairy tales promised I would someday find my own Prince Charming. I hoped I would experience a "sweep you off your feet" kind of love with a man who would surpass my wildest expectations.

Of course, I imagined having my father walk me down the aisle. And as the images of my wedding gown changed over the years, since high school, there has only been one person I ever imagined as my groom. Today, when I look back, I consider myself incredibly blessed to say I married my best friend: Jeffrey Baurer.

My husband, Jeff, and I first crossed paths as young children. He grew up blocks away from the ball fields of the Christian Center and would ride his bike over to play Little League baseball, while I spent my summers there playing girls' softball. Jeff's sister was even on my team for one year. Truth be told, I have no memory of ever not knowing him. Looking back on our childhood, I can honestly say that we had a rather ideal upbringing, growing up in the safety and comfort of Peoria, Illinois. Just shy of a three-hour trek from Chicago, we were blessed to have most of what we ever needed. Jeff was born the older of two and the only son of a furniture store owner and school teacher. He was followed four years later by his sister, Kimberly.

Growing up the baby of five meant I had all the support and nurturing I needed. Part of what makes my family so interesting is the story of my parents, which, like most good stories, is really a love story. While not always perfect, it definitely made an impact on my perception of the world and influenced my view on marriage and family.

My parents were married the first week after their college graduation from Knox College in June 1953. My dad was in the ROTC and was commissioned as a second lieutenant upon graduation. He was sent to Fort Benning in Georgia for training before moving to Fort Ord in California. It was there that my dad re-enlisted and was accepted into flight school. He was already a pilot, having become the youngest person in Illinois to earn his license, while still in high school.

Gary Air Force Base in San Marcos, Texas, became their home for his first year of flight training. My mom flew home to Davenport, Iowa, from Texas to give birth to my sister, Marilyn, in September 1954. With their newborn infant in tow, my parents moved to Fort Rucker in Alabama for my dad to finish flight school. He was then assigned to the 11th Airborne Division at Fort Campbell, Kentucky. It was with the 11th Airborne that my parents were sent to Augsburg, Germany, in February 1956.

When my parents returned from Germany, my mom was already expecting baby number two. My sister, Anne, was born in December 1957. The next year, after being married for five years, my parents divorced while my dad was attending law school at Indiana University. It was a crushing blow for both of them. However, as fate would have it, they remarried in 1963, determined to continue their dream of having a large family.

My mom and two sisters moved to Peoria where my dad was already practicing law. In the spring of 1967, my brother, Gregg, was born. Two years later, my parents were expecting baby number four, due to arrive in the summer of 1969. In June, my mother's sister, startled by my mother's size, suggested she be reexamined to confirm the due date. The obstetrician, a friend of my parents, was certain that their fourth child would be a hefty baby boy. On the evening of August 19, as my mother was being wheeled into the delivery room, her doctor, so confident of his assessment, proclaimed he would waive his fee if she did not deliver at least a nine-and-a-half-pound baby boy.

But, boy, was he wrong!

My sister Marcia and I came into the world slightly late, as my mom's labor had to be medically induced. Marcia Claire arrived first, weighing in at an even seven pounds. My mom remembers hearing the doctor declare a girl as my dad was quickly ushered out of the delivery room. I had to be turned to be delivered safely, and my mother was immediately sedated. At six pounds, three ounces, I arrived exactly seven minutes later—and our delivery was absolutely free. The hefty boy that was expected was actually a set of identical twin girls with a combined weight of over thirteen pounds.

I was immediately named Margaret Jean. Margaret is after my mother's only sister, and Jean is a nod to my paternal grandfather, Eugene, who was known to all as Gene. My grandfather, who had a fraternal twin brother, loved to take credit for our birth, noting that most twin births skip a generation.

"Bonus Baby" became my nickname from the very start. I continue to take full advantage of every opportunity to remind my siblings of the bonus and blessing that I am. I take great pride in pointing out that after four tries, God came close to perfection with Marcia but struck divine completion with me! As kids growing up in the 1970s at the height of *Brady Bunch* fame, my brother and twin were armed with the perfect—and somewhat devastating—comeback. After all, their names were Gregg and Marcia, and according to them, if I were indeed that special, I would have been named Jan or Cindy.

Marcia and I were identical in every sense of the word. Some family members struggled to tell us apart, especially as infants. My mom and two-and-a-half-year-old brother had no trouble at all. My dad, however, found it a challenge. Unwilling to rely on the word of a toddler, who was always undeniably correct, my dad had us wear ankle bracelets engraved with our names. It was later determined that not only are Marcia and I identical, but we are also considered mirror-image twins. Nearly a quarter of all identical twins face each other in the womb. We are thought to be reflections of each other, with the same yet sometimes opposite features. In our case, Marcia is left-handed, while I am right-handed.

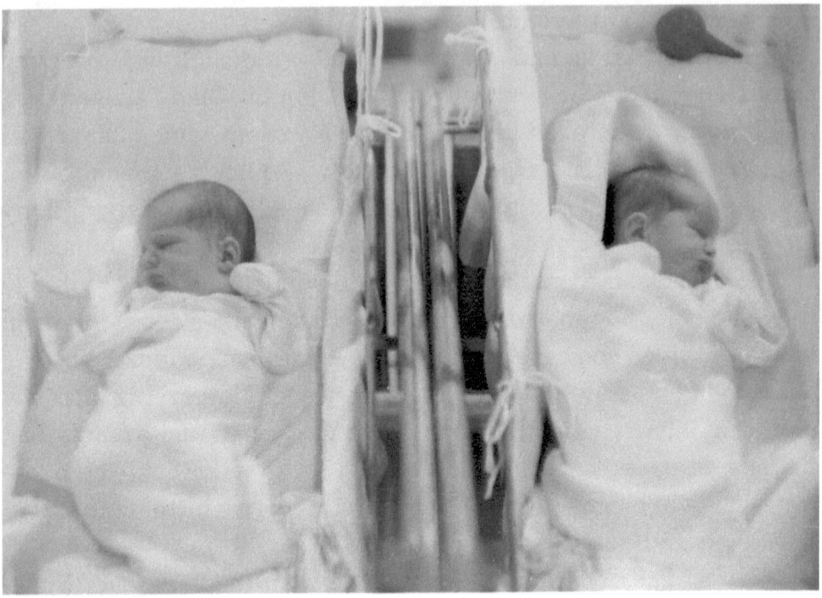

(L–R) Marcia Claire and Margaret Jean—August 1969

My grandmother suggested that because we were always together, it might be a good idea to allow us to have "worldly" experiences separate from one another. My mom began to take one twin to the grocery store while leaving the other at home. Although a wonderful idea, separating the two of us did not work. The twin at the store yelled, "Where's baby?" as the twin at home cried the same thing. "Baby" was one of our first words, but understanding our speech was as challenging as telling us apart. To onlookers, we babbled a proprietary blend of gibberish. But to us, our "Twinnish"—a term coined by our dad—was a real language. My mom and brother were the only ones who understood us, and translating what Marcia and I were saying became a full-time job for my toddler brother.

At age three, Marcia and I were off to Peter Pan Preschool. Of course, we were immediately flagged as requiring speech intervention. Still, our beloved preschool teacher assured my parents that our speech would improve as we were forced to speak correctly to communicate with our friends in our classroom. She also encouraged our family at home to respond to the two of us only when we spoke standard English.

The Johnson Family (Marilyn, Gregg, Anne, Margaret, Mom, Dad, and Marcia)—1975

Childhood was an idyllic, carefree time, and I loved every stage. I loved going to school, had a lot of fun playing on various teams, and enjoyed high school's increased responsibilities and social obligations. I always wanted my children to have the same picture-perfect experience. Despite my parents' second divorce in 1982, I thought the world was wonderful. I wasn't naive to bad things, but they didn't seem to enter my orbit or dampen my spirits. I firmly believed that things usually worked out as they should, and I was very happy and content to be living in my own *pink sky, bluegrass world.* I never considered how my life could starkly contrast with that of my peers.

As a twin, Marcia went through every transition with me. I had a partner in crime, and she was my most trusted confidant. We were both taught by our parents that if you work hard, more often than not you will achieve what you want. Though we looked alike on the outside, Marcia and I each had two very distinct personalities. We dressed alike almost daily until about fifth grade. Marcia probably would have continued this tradition longer, but I was ready to start expressing our differences. I was always talkative, while she was a little shyer and reserved. We would be stopped at the mall and asked if we were twins. Marcia would look at me, and I knew I was expected to respond. So that's what I did.

Even though I was affectionately known as "the baby," because I was the more outgoing of the two of us, I became the leader. Marcia was more of a homebody. I would make the plans, and once all arrangements were made, she would then happily join. As the instigator, I was the one who pushed her to take risks and step outside of her comfort zone. At the same time, she reined me in just enough to keep me safe from any severe consequences. I think we both would agree that we were and are the perfect balance for each other. Despite our personality differences, however, we were able to experience some trademark traits of *twinning.*

Our voices sounded nearly identical, especially on the phone, so we took advantage of this when it was helpful to either one of us. Cell phones did not exist when we were in seventh and eighth grade, and there was no such thing as "snapping" or texting one of our latest crushes. When I was "going with" a boy, we talked to each other in class and then on the phone every night. When it came to breaking up over the phone, having a twin with a voice exactly like your own made things much easier. I am quite certain Marcia never broke up with a boy before high school because I usually did it for her.

But switching places was even more fun than breaking up with my twin sister's boyfriends. Our academic abilities were almost identical, so while taking honors classes, we were sometimes placed in the same class. Our friends in high school knew our personalities well and encouraged us to switch seats to get the teacher's head spinning, trying to figure out why something did not feel right. After the switch, we would intentionally raise our hands for the sake of getting called the wrong names in class. With even more prodding from our friends, I would ask absurd questions to make Marcia look ridiculous. As much as we were willing to switch seats in a classroom, we never took a test for the other. Not only was the thought of getting in trouble not appealing, but our handwriting was also *very* different. We used the opposite hand, so it would have been a dead giveaway.

As little girls, Marcia and I were very active, playing sports outside with our brother and with all the neighborhood kids. We especially loved to play softball. Our house was on Stephen Drive, and we lived directly across the street from the entrance of Susan Curve. The end of our driveway was home plate, with second base and center field straight up the street in the middle of Susan Curve. We became quite competitive trying to keep up with our brother and the older boys in the neighborhood. We attended one elementary school, Rolling Acres, from kindergarten through eighth grade. Beginning in fifth grade, we ran track and played basketball, volleyball, and softball. We both then became cheerleaders in seventh and eighth grades. I cannot overstate the sense of school spirit and pride that develops when attending one school from K–8. We were the Cougars, recognized not only for our athletics but also for our supportive parents and fans, who donned the red and white and cheered loudly at every sporting event.

We had an intense rivalry with another elementary school. Although we did not face them in regular conference play, we often met in city tournaments. They were the Wildcats from Washington. They were not only talented athletes but also academically gifted. Students from across the district were tested at the end of third grade. If accepted, they could attend the Gifted Program at Washington for the remainder of their elementary years, grades four through eight. Jeff was a student at Washington. He shared this comradery with my sister Anne, who had also attended Washington years before. They later loved to tout their perceived superior intellect during family gatherings and holidays.

Although I knew Jeff from summer softball at the Christian Center, I remember talking to him for the first time after a very competitive Rolling Acres vs. Washington girls' game. It's funny because I don't remember who won that game, but I can still see him standing on the hill next to the diamond wearing Washington's blue and gold. He was on my turf, as it was our home game, and was extraordinarily complimentary of my play. This was absolutely no surprise. He was always so considerate. He did not want the girls hiding alone after dark when he came over to play neighborhood tag. He possessed traits not typical of a young teenage boy. As I think back, even then, he gave his full attention to whomever he was with. He respectfully spoke directly to parents, not in an "Eddie Haskell" way but with a genuineness that I cannot even put into words. It is for these reasons that my mom always trusted him.

Although Jeff played many sports throughout his childhood, his main sport was hockey. At a time in the early 1980s when each sport had a "season" and actually stopped and started, Jeff was traveling with his various elite hockey teams. I considered myself quite athletic, but when it came to ice, snow, and water, Jeff could not be touched. To a young teenage girl, his speed on the ice and his ability to come to a complete stop in one swift motion on the edges of both skates never failed to impress.

(Later, as an adult, he would show the same dazzle on skis. As I was trying to master the snowplow, he would be racing down a black diamond and throwing snow in my direction as he came to a hockey-style stop. In addition, the rooster tails he created while slalom water-skiing on Long Lake are still legendary to our children.)

Until my junior year and Jeff's senior year, we were just wonderful friends. We ran around in the same friend group and saw each other constantly. He even seriously dated some of my good friends. But regardless of who we were dating, we remained friends always. In fact, I enjoyed our friendship so much that I never really considered dating him at that age. Jeff and I could talk—and I mean really talk—about anything and everything.

Honestly, I have no idea when my romantic feelings developed for Jeff. I don't recall it being a singular moment, but rather a gradual build-up over time. I have no recollection of him not being a part of my world. He was in my neighborhood and stopped by when heading to his friend's house down the street from us. I was a bit naive about the true nature of our friendship. My mother recognized it long before I did. If she knew Jeff Baurer would be at the party, I didn't have a curfew. She knew that I was in good hands and would get home safely and on time. Not many daughters can say that about their moms when spending unchaperoned time with teenage boys!

Genuine romantic interest between us became palpable in the spring of 1986, but it was only casual at best. Our very first date would be at the Glen Oak Zoo. Next, and long before junior and senior boys faced the intense pressure to find the most creative way to invite a girl to a dance, Jeff asked me to his senior prom. No, I did not receive a pizza with pepperoni forming the letters P-R-O-M—"promposals" weren't a thing back then—but I did receive a phone call while babysitting for my neighbors. It was simple, but it was sweet.

I was a junior class officer, so I spent nearly the entire Saturday of prom decorating the ballroom of the downtown Peoria hotel hosting our dance. I remember having very little time to get ready, and Jeff would be punctual to the minute. He picked me up in a red convertible. We took pictures at my house first, but Jeff was distraught, as he had left my corsage in his refrigerator. We returned to his house for pictures and to pick up the corsage. Without even a thought, he headed back to my house so my mom could take more pictures of me with my flowers. I attended a few homecoming and vice-versa (aka Sadie Hawkins) dances, but I remember Jeff's senior prom the most. We ended up spending quite a bit of time apart supporting two of our good friends who decided to break up during the dance. (It's not truly a prom night unless at least one popular couple breaks up, right?) Following the dance, while many of our classmates were drinking in the hotel's guest rooms, our large group was being chased by the local authorities after we'd decided to go to the school and engage in a water-balloon fight.

As luck would have it, Jeff and I broke up a couple weeks later over a misunderstanding at our school's spring musical. (Years later, and after we'd gotten back together and were married, we still did not agree on what had caused this breakup.) However, we remained the best of friends that summer. With Jeff going off to college in a few months, it was easier to let him go than to try to date him again. Although many high-school couples and even close friends end up never speaking to each other again after graduation, going off to college only intensified our friendship. With so many exciting changes on the horizon, we were both eager to see what the future would hold.

Chapter 2

MARGARET

Although Jeff and I are considered to have been "high-school sweethearts," the truth is our relationship took time before we matured into a full-blown couple. It wasn't until well after high school when we slowly blossomed into something more than friends. It was a gradual process that took honesty, communication, and trust—and as we grew closer, we had a lot of fun along the way.

Transitioning from a high-school senior to a college freshman is challenging for any eighteen-year-old. Yet, as our personalities and sense of independence changed as we got older, our friendship remained constant. Our relationship was always easy, and it became effortless as the years passed. Despite breaking up when Jeff went off to college, he and I maintained a strong, unbreakable bond.

As I went into my senior year and Jeff began his first year away from home, we each fell into a natural rhythm of living our own lives. He would write to me from Iowa State, where he was enrolled in the College of Engineering. I loved getting letters from Jeff. He shared his excitement for his fraternity and on-campus events and a new crush he was taking to a dance. I was never jealous (that would come later). At this point, we were both pursuing our own interests and experiencing our own freedom. However, there was much comfort in knowing Jeff was *there*. He not only felt safe; he was safe. It was unspoken, but we understood that we had each other's back. *Always*. This type of trust takes time to develop, and we reveled in the security of having a trustworthy friend with whom we could share anything and everything.

During my first year away at DePauw University in Greencastle, Indiana, Jeff was still enjoying his fraternity and all that Iowa State had to offer. Two years into his degree, however, he decided to make the switch from the rigors of engineering to a business degree, transferring to Bradley University in our hometown of Peoria. He moved into a house near the campus, transferred his fraternity membership of Pi Kappa Alpha (Pike) to the Bradley chapter and began working full time at his father's store. With Jeff now living in Peoria, we had a lot of fun, especially during the summer. His house, just off Main Street near the university, had a very large porch across the front. I remember spending many summer nights on that porch with his roommates and friends. I give Jeff and a couple others full credit for teaching me how to drink. I will forever have an affinity for *Milwaukee's Best,* our beer of choice back in the day.

With a fall birthday, Jeff was very young for his grade. During the summer of 1989, neither Jeff nor I were of legal drinking age. I will never forget exactly where I sat on Jeff's porch the night I saw two squad cars turn onto Jeff's street and speed toward his house with their lights flashing. I remember yelling, "Run!" as Jeff grabbed my hand to charge up the stairs to his third-floor bedroom—with Marcia in tow. We were the only three people there who were underage, so his roommates remained outside to talk to the officers. They had seen us run, so while they were searching for us in the yard, Jeff, Marcia, and I were on the third floor rinsing our mouths out with Listerine—*as if doing so was beneficial in any way.* Unable to enter the premises without a warrant, the officers left before discovering our whereabouts.

Although Jeff and I were not dating during this time, our friendship continued to deepen. His parents had separated, and he confided that he was struggling to process their pending divorce. Putting our trust and comfort into words, even now, is difficult. Jeff was family, almost like a protective big brother. He did not need an invitation to come over to my house. He was always welcome, any time. I could almost *do no wrong* when Jeff was present. My mother may not appreciate my sharing the following story, but I feel it clearly illustrates my point. It is also a story that has been told and retold many times with laughter in the past three decades.

Jeff and several of our friends were at my house during Christmas break. Marcia and I were the only girls at the kitchen table. We were also the only two who had not yet turned twenty-one. My mom, Anne, and my brother-in-law arrived home to find us playing Speed Quarters (a drinking game). Before Marcia and I had time to consider whether we were in trouble, the three pulled up chairs and joined us. I was seated next to Jeff, and he made sure my mom sat to his right. He protected her all evening from getting caught with both cups and having to *pound* a full glass of beer. Both Marcia and Anne loved to remind Jeff of all the *brownnosing* that occurred that night. In fact, one of the other guys at the table that evening who had been flirting with me at one point said, "I don't even know why I'm bothering to ask you out because you are going to marry Jeff Baurer anyway." I considered Jeff to be like a brother to me—and truth be told, I struggled to get past this for a long time. We did not cross a romantic line until we both found ourselves living and working in the Windy City.

One of the unexpected "benefits" of Jeff transferring to Bradley was that he lost a year, which meant we would be graduating at the same time. In the fall of 1990, months before graduation, Jeff had already accepted an offer from Andersen Consulting in Chicago. One of the qualities I admired most about Jeff was his drive. He was always well prepared and never shied away from hard work. I was not the least bit surprised that he had secured employment well before graduation.

I, however, was not nearly as diligent as Jeff was regarding the job search. I was interviewing on campus and was certain I wanted to move to Chicago, but finding employment before graduation was not my priority. I was soaking up all the "lasts" of my final semester at DePauw. I had pledged Pi Beta Phi as a freshman and was enjoying senior dinners, spring formals, and the decreased responsibility of no longer holding an executive office in the sorority house. During our final semester, Jeff and I did not keep in touch. I knew Jeff was moving to Chicago, but I did not know his exact plans.

Before college graduation, I was not overly concerned with Jeff's dating life, and I had no problem discussing it with him. But I did *not* like hearing about who he was dating when we were both residing in

Chicago. (I was living in the western suburbs with Anne and her family during my job search.) One of his first projects was in Kansas City, Missouri, where he would work during the week and then fly back almost every weekend. He reached out to me and would occasionally come out to the suburbs. I knew that I was starting to have feelings for him when he began to tell me about meeting an airline attendant during one of his flights to Kansas City. I had just started to work for a real-estate developer in the Loop and had moved to my own apartment in a suburb just west of the city. Although Jeff and I saw quite a bit of each other that summer, our first actual date wasn't until that fall. Jeff's roommate's girlfriend was visiting from out of state and he wanted me to meet her, so he asked if I wanted to go to Second City, a world-renowned comedy club in Chicago. Second City is where many comedians go to get their start and, ironically enough, is where Jeff and I started our romantic relationship.

Jeff and I had a great time together for the next several months. He continued to fly back and forth to Kansas City, and I made many new friends at work. During the summer of 1992, one of my best work friends and I helped put together a company softball team. I had just turned twenty-three, was gainfully employed, and was having a blast in the city. Jeff flew me to Kansas City early that fall to meet his friends working on his project. His apartment was located just off Country Club Plaza. He couldn't wait to take me to the many shops in Crown Center and introduce me to Kansas City's authentic barbecue.

Jeff was absolutely the perfect host. He was generous and really took care of me and everyone with us. He always thought of me first and himself last. Jeff did not treat me this way just while I was visiting; this was who Jeff was every day. If someone had to face the kitchen at a restaurant, Jeff would immediately switch seats. He always took the worst seat, especially if it was underneath a vent blowing freezing-cold air during the entire meal. Jeff made a special effort to notice the nametag of our server, and then he called that person by name the whole evening. Jeff was the guy who always opened the door for other people. He never failed to push me to the inside so that he was closest to the street when we would walk in the city. Once when we were pulling out of a parking lot during a rainstorm, Jeff noticed an elderly woman walking out of the restaurant. Without hesitation, Jeff pulled the car over. He jumped out with an umbrella and escorted her to her automobile. This was Jeff Baurer.

Jeff was a picture-perfect gentleman, a dream suitor for any parent's daughter. My issue was that he was very serious at this point. I was silently struggling to get past our best-friend status and extraordinarily concerned about losing him permanently if we did not work out as a couple. He told me in Kansas City that he could see our entire future—complete with a house with a white picket fence and children. I was fresh out of college, earning a paycheck, and focused on having the most fun in a city I loved. Jeff was talking about settling down; he was always planning ahead. He was there, but that's not where I was—yet.

For weeks following a trip to visit Jeff, I tried to wrap my head around all his future plans for us. I continued to question whether I should stay in our relationship when I was not feeling as strongly as he was. The week between Christmas and New Year's, Jeff was becoming frustrated by what he considered a lack of commitment on my part. He was so frustrated, in fact, that he forced me into making a very quick decision, one that I was not quite ready to make.

He flew in from Kansas City for a couple days before New Year's and met me at a bar with my coworkers. He had just walked in the door and insisted we leave to be alone. It was still early evening, and I was not ready to leave my friends. As minor as this may sound, it was significant because it led to our first and only very public argument. He took my hand and started to lead me to the door. I dropped his hand and was just as insistent that I was not leaving. We argued, and he walked out and jumped into a cab to head back to his apartment. I knew he was sure I would follow, but I didn't.

He and his roommates were hosting a New Year's Eve party the next night. We both needed to cool off, but in his mind, there was no question I would be at his party. I am ashamed to admit I did not attend. This was long before cell phones and texting, so he called me early the next day to find out what had happened to me. It was New Year's Day, January 1, 1993, and during this phone call, I ended our relationship. After I returned to work, a friend, who had witnessed my argument with Jeff at the bar, asked me if all was well between us. When I told him we had broken up, he instantly shot back, "I don't know why you're wasting time apart because I can tell you, you're going to marry that guy."

I began 1993 slightly relieved and with a new sense of freedom. I ceased all communication with Jeff to give us the space I believed we needed. I casually dated that spring and summer. A friend at work set me up with her husband's coworker. We had fun, but I knew this relationship would never be serious. Life in the city was great, and I thought that I was moving forward, until six months later when I received a phone call from someone asking for "Stephanie."

Instantly, I knew the voice. I was immediately pissed and retorted, "Who in the hell is Stephanie?" He had intended to call his friend, whose wife was named Stephanie, but had inadvertently dialed the only other number with a 708 area code he had committed to memory. "Oh my God, Margaret?" was Jeff's response. He then said it had been so long since he had heard from me that he was considering calling my mother to make sure I had not gotten hit by a city bus. This accidental phone call turned into a two-hour conversation. During our call, we discovered that we had both read *The Firm*, and the movie was about to be released. We made plans to see the movie together "as friends" with no expectations.

He picked me up in LaGrange, and we saw the movie in Oak Brook. During most of our dating relationship, Jeff would drive from the city to my apartment in LaGrange, and then we would head back to the city to go out with friends. He would then usually make this round-trip drive again at the end of the evening to take me home. It became more than a joke when Jeff would tell the story about his close relationship with the gas-station attendant in LaGrange, where he would stop to fill up his car and buy a coffee. But this time, after the movie, I invited Jeff to spend the night on my couch, which opened the door to rekindling our relationship.

My family cautioned me about communicating with Jeff again unless I was serious this time. They warned me not to hurt him. Jeff took me to a Cubs game to celebrate my birthday a couple weeks later. There was absolutely no doubt that I was one-hundred-percent committed after this game. He may have been all-in first, but now I was too. Knowing what I know now, I would never have wasted those seven months apart. Years later, Jeff and I would affectionately refer to this time as my "insanity period." I would kill to have this time back. However, I genuinely believe I had to be without him to truly appreciate what we had when we were together.

Over the next year together, our relationship continued to thrive, and we were gearing up for a wonderful holiday season. Christmas Eve has always been a special holiday for my family, but Christmas Eve 1994 will forever be the most magical one for me. The year before, Jeff had started a tradition of sending a small gift to each of my nieces and nephews that "Santa Claus" would hand-deliver to them. Santa Claus was actually Jeff's former elementary-school principal, who dressed up to surprise the children of his close family friends. For my nieces and nephews, this small gift was a preview of what would come when Santa came back down the chimney later that night.

Inside Santa's bag of goodies this year was also a special gift for me. As an avid Disney fan, to say that my gift was enchanting would be an understatement. I unwrapped a copy of *Snow White and the Seven Dwarfs*, which had just been released for the first time on VHS. As it was one of my favorite fairy tales of all time, I was instantly impressed with Jeff's thoughtful gift. However, this was no ordinary copy. On the outside was a sticky note, which intrigued me.

Inscribed on the note, Jeff had written, "Everyone knows how the story ends . . . " I did not initially notice that the cellophane had been removed from the VHS, and poking out from the top of the video case was a curly red ribbon. Curious about the sticky note, I pulled the case open to reveal the movie video with yet another sticky note on the top inscribed with the words, "We live happily ever after . . ." followed by an arrow pointing to the other side of the case, where, hanging from the curly red ribbon, was the most beautiful diamond ring I'd ever seen. Jeff was proposing with my entire family standing around me, and a tipped-off Marcia waiting in the wings with champagne.

Two days after Christmas, Jeff and I met several of our couple friends in Breckinridge, Colorado, to spend a week skiing and celebrating the new year. While in Colorado and with the help of my mother to secure the church and a venue, our wedding date was set for November 4, 1995.

My twin sister Marcia was already engaged and set to marry in April. As a matter of fact, Marcia was also marrying a man named Jeff. My sister Anne had already married a man named Jeff. We tended to identify our "Jeffs" by referring to them as either "my" Jeff or "her" Jeff. To clarify, it soon became customary for Anne, Marcia, and me to call them by their last name—Harris, Clark, and Baurer, respectively. It also became customary for them to argue who was the "original" or even "favorite" Jeff.

Since Marcia and I were getting married in the same year, some friends suggested we have a double wedding. We already shared a birthday, so we really didn't want to share our wedding day and all future anniversaries. With my date set and being Marcia's maid of honor, I focused entirely on hosting a bridal shower and planning her bachelorette party leading up to her big day. This was a very special time for Marcia. My time was yet to come.

I returned to work on Monday following Marcia's wedding weekend. Sitting on my desk when I walked in was a large bouquet of red roses with a note from Jeff. It simply read, "Now is your time to be queen." With Marcia and Jeff Clark enjoying a honeymoon in Hawaii, the focus turned to Jeff and me. It was now my turn. There were showers and luncheons to plan, and lots of wedding details to finalize. We had exactly seven months to do it, and I couldn't wait.

I'd always envisioned my wedding happening on a crisp fall evening as the leaves were changing colors. Our ceremony in Peoria was not until early evening, so our wedding day opened with a large family brunch hosted by my aunt and uncle. This was a perfect way for Jeff and me to spend time with family and out-of-town guests, as we knew we would not have this time during the reception.

We could not have been more thrilled with our day. It was exactly as we'd planned and hoped it would be—surrounded by family and friends from our childhood and life in Chicago. It had become customary for

Mr. and Mrs. Jeffrey W. Baurer—
November 4, 1995

family and friends to play pranks on the bride and groom. Toilet paper and towels were typically stolen from the bridal suite. Soap dispensers were switched out with peppermint-scented toothpaste, or the bed was stripped of pillows and sheets. The car might be filled with balloons with chains locked to the back bumper.

Jeff and I had to drive back to Chicago the day after our wedding to catch an international flight on Monday morning. To avoid any cleanup a potential prank might require, we safely tucked our car away in Jeff's great aunt's garage before the brunch. Although we were registered to stay in the bridal suite at our venue, we had secretly registered under assumed names at a separate hotel. We had no car, so my father-in-law played along by driving us to our hotel. He actually picked us up in the alley, and he escorted me in my full bridal gown and Jeff in a tux to an off-site location across the river where no one would think to look for us.

Our honeymoon was in St. Lucia, and not even a six-hour flight delay or having our luggage lost could diminish our excitement. We relaxed and enjoyed the beautiful beachfront terrain, where we met several other newlywed couples. I am still in touch with a few of them today. One couple we met had gotten married on the beach, and we were their wedding guests. We spent two weeks on the beach, in the pool, and eating in amazing restaurants. We were even chosen to compete in a version of the *Newlywed Game* at our resort. Growing up together probably gave us an unfair advantage, as we walked away the clear winners, not missing a single question.

Jeff and I returned from our honeymoon just before Thanksgiving, so we immediately jumped into the holiday season. From our wedding day through Christmas, the first few weeks of our marriage were full of work parties and family festivities. As the new year approached, we could not wait to really start our married life in our new apartment on Lake Shore Drive in Chicago.

Chapter 3

MARGARET

After spending the first year of our marriage in a Chicago high-rise on Lake Shore Drive, we settled in Geneva, Illinois. We purchased our first home in December 1996 in a neighborhood full of other young couples and families. I hadn't a clue in which boxes we might find our towels and toiletries, but rest assured, we had a real and fully decorated Christmas tree in our family room within the first couple days. Jeff was working at his dream job with Accenture (formerly Andersen Consulting) and had no plans of leaving his hard-earned role there. He was promoted to manager while working "on the line," meaning he worked directly with clients on-site. Although his position afforded him all the perks he could ever want, Jeff also had to travel *a lot*.

Two years into our marriage, I became pregnant with our first child. My coworkers surprised me with a baby shower on April 17, 1998, a Friday night. The next day, my twin sister and my best friend were hosting a large baby shower for me in Naperville. Everyone was working around the clock to ensure my shower would be special. My mom was already in town, and she and Marcia were staying at Anne's, where the shower was being held. I was excited to see my family and spend time with them before the baby arrived. With my due date about five weeks away, we had the nursery almost ready, and my lifelong dream of becoming a mother was finally becoming a reality. As I went to sleep that night, I thought about nothing except waking up early to prepare for my shower.

What started out as a peaceful night's sleep turned into an emergency. I woke up to excruciating back pain at 2:30 a.m. Jeff immediately wanted to call the doctor's emergency line. I protested because I wasn't due for at least another month. Jeff took one look at me and knew this was no false alarm. With the phone already in his hand, he began to dial.

Jeff got the on-call doctor on the line and started to explain that I was experiencing unbearable back pain. The doctor had no interest in speaking to Jeff and insisted I get on the phone. As soon as the doctor heard my frazzled voice, he knew I was in labor. He instructed us to get in our car and to the hospital as quickly as possible.

The irony of the situation was not only that I was going into labor on the day of my baby shower but also that there was a hospital at the entrance of our subdivision. Jeff had wanted us to choose that hospital in case something like this happened, but I persisted and chose the hospital with the obstetrician I loved and a NICU (neonatal intensive care unit). As we drove past the nearby hospital, Jeff asked me again why we were driving an extra thirty minutes to another hospital. I reminded him that our hospital had a crisis nursery, although actually needing it never entered my mind.

Jeff and I arrived at the hospital sleep-deprived yet wide awake from adrenaline at 4:30 a.m. I called Anne, who woke up my mom and Marcia to let them know that I was going into labor and would definitely not be at the shower. They called my other sister Marilyn, who joined them around Anne's kitchen table at 5:00 a.m. for coffee while they awaited news from me. They also decided to still host the event because it was too late to call everyone and cancel.

The labor and delivery nurse accurately predicted that our baby would arrive by 7:30 a.m. As if right on cue, at 7:27 a.m., Sarah Jo arrived weighing six pounds, ten ounces. I saw her for about one second before she was whisked away. Jeff and I were both startled by how quickly our rather calm three-hour labor had turned into an intense and chaotic few minutes following Sarah's arrival. Because I was delivering a month early, a neonatologist was also present. Seeing that I was visibly upset, he reassured me by saying, "If this baby was my own daughter, I would not be worried because she is practically a full-grown teenager compared to the other babies in the NICU."

Meanwhile, Marcia stood in for me and opened all my baby-shower gifts while I was recovering from the delivery. My mom left the baby shower and came to the hospital to support me. Periodically, I'd get updates from the party. Once I was in my hospital room, they even passed the phone around so I could talk to everyone there.

Later that day, I was wheeled into the nursery to see our precious, new baby girl. Sarah was hooked up to an entire wall of machines. Still, I immediately realized how blessed we were because Sarah was massive compared to the other babies. They needed to keep her in the NICU for five days, so Jeff and I were discharged without her. With my newborn in the hospital, it was difficult for me to sleep knowing that I couldn't be there with her. I'll never forget the moment we finally got to take her home for the very first time!

To celebrate our fourth wedding anniversary, Jeff and I planned a weekend trip to Door County, Wisconsin, also known as the "Cape Cod of the Midwest." We could not have been more excited about the picturesque views of exploding fall colors. We had just discovered that our second baby was on the way. But upon our arrival at the resort, I knew something was very wrong.

Just eighteen months after Sarah was born, I suffered my first miscarriage. I was consumed by the pain of losing that pregnancy. Sarah, sensing my devastation, would crawl over to me and gently pat me to offer her sympathy.

After many months of failed attempts to conceive again, Jeff and I wondered if something could be wrong. We sought the guidance of a renowned specialist. After significant testing, Jeff and I discovered that we both had fertility issues. At first, we tried all the easy, quick fixes the doctors recommended, but to no avail. I was very unwilling to waste any more time, so our specialist agreed to come out with all guns blazing. We tried three rounds of in-vitro fertilization (IVF). The first transfer didn't work, which left me shattered and our doctor confused, as he'd considered me a perfect candidate. The second transfer was successful but ended with another devastating loss. Jeff and I were hopeful that our third time would be the charm. It was, but during a routine exam in the summer of 2001, they could not find a heartbeat, and I miscarried for the third and final time. They ran extensive tests, and we sought a second opinion from another fertility specialist. That specialist sent us to yet another specialist, who, in August 2001, came back with the diagnosis of reproductive autoimmune failure syndrome. We were crushed.

The only silver lining was that my diagnosis only affected the reproductive system. The bad news, however, is that it affects the *reproductive system*. My diagnosis was complicated. I had an elevated white-blood-cell count, and the killing activity of those cells was also elevated. After hearing what we considered risky treatment options, Jeff and I left the hospital determined to start the adoption process.

I was overwhelmed by the thought of researching adoption. However, I had spent the past two years very much in tune with my body, so the thought of moving forward without daily injections and blood draws was almost a relief. As we started to share with our loved ones that we were looking into adoption, a friend put me in touch with their friend who had just successfully adopted their second child. This connection ultimately resulted in the hiring of our adoption attorney.

So many channels and procedures must be followed to the letter to even qualify for adoption. We were encouraged to become involved with as many adoption centers as financially reasonable to increase our chances of finding a baby. We started our search close to home in Chicago. Jeff and I completed all of the necessary evening classes, mountains of paperwork, and extensive home studies that were required.

After completing all the requirements in Illinois, we contacted the adoption attorney, who lived and practiced in Arkansas. He mailed us a DVD that walked us through the Arkansas process from start to finish. Shortly after watching the video, we mailed him our completed paperwork and officially engaged him to help us adopt a baby.

In January 2002, we decided to make the nine-hour drive to meet our attorney and get the ball rolling. His service included placing ads in newspapers across Arkansas describing us to potential birth mothers looking to find parents for their unborn children. We then installed an 800 number for birth mothers to call if they were interested in responding to our ad.

We had a glossy white phone installed on our kitchen wall. If that white phone rang, our hearts dropped into the basement, knowing a potential birth mother could be on the other end. Our attorney had prepared us for having only a twenty-percent chance of a birth mother reaching out to us directly on the phone as a result of the ads. It was much more likely that he would personally match us with a birth mother who had contacted his firm on her own. Jeff and I had no idea into which category we might fall.

Within the first couple weeks following installation, our white phone rang a few times. It was disappointing to hear the tone of a fax machine as someone had misdialed. It was even more disappointing each time we heard the demoralizing echo of a dial tone because of a hang-up. Then, on a very chilly Friday afternoon on the twenty-second of February, I picked up our phone and heard the voice of a young woman with a thick, Southern accent. After sharing her name, she mentioned our ad and admitted that she had been calling and hanging up. I immediately sympathized with her when she shared that she had been the one doing that because she kept losing her nerve. Our voices trembled. I remember admitting that I was as terrified as she was and suggested we start by sharing a little about each other. Her vulnerability, sincerity, and willingness to share her story honestly stunned me.

I put a Barney movie in the VCR for Sarah and replayed it several times as I talked to our potential birth mother for more than two hours. Jeff was working in the suburbs and came home for lunch that afternoon. When he walked in, he looked like a deer in headlights when he saw me talking with someone on our white phone.

As soon as I hung up the receiver, I relayed to Jeff every detail of my conversation with the woman, who had ended our call by saying,

"Margaret, I want you and Jeff to adopt my baby." I then called our adoption attorney, who was out of town meeting with other clients roughly five hours away from the birth mother's home. The woman had agreed to meet, so our attorney jumped into his car and drove to her house. Time was of the essence, as he wanted to confirm that she was indeed thirty weeks pregnant and verify her intention to place her baby for adoption right away. He instructed us to plan to meet her as soon as possible.

The birth mother and our attorney met at 8:00 p.m. that evening, and not even an hour later, she called me and excitedly told me about it. It had hardly been eight hours since I'd received this young mother's call, and I was now talking to her for the third time and making plans to meet her the next day. My mom and Marcia agreed to care for Sarah, so Jeff and I packed up and headed to Peoria. We arrived just after midnight and began our more than ten-hour drive to Arkansas at 5:00 a.m. on Saturday, February 23, 2002.

Our attorney had difficulty finding the birth mother's home the night before and suggested we meet her at a restaurant. We made plans to meet at Applebee's in El Dorado, Arkansas, at 4:30 p.m. The closer Jeff and I got to the restaurant, the more nervous I became. Jeff was very relaxed, and I knew he would help carry our conversation with the woman and smooth over any awkward silences. Sitting there with my husband and the potential biological mother of our next child was an awkward experience, to say the very least. We made small talk and polite conversation, and were a bit relieved when our meals arrived quickly. I began worrying about what we would do after dinner, but as we walked to our cars, she put my fear to rest by suggesting the three of us go to the hospital where she was planning to deliver the baby.

I will never forget entering the hospital lobby and watching her march to the information desk. With absolute confidence, she explained that Jeff and I were from out of town and would be adopting her baby, and she would like to give us a tour of the maternity ward. The woman at the desk was very gracious and told us to take all the time we needed. It was now early evening, and we talked for a little longer in the hospital parking lot before we headed back to

Illinois. This was the only time we saw the birth mother until after the baby was born.

With ten weeks to go before her due date, she would contact us two to three times per week to let us know how her pregnancy was progressing. She did not seem to have much family support, so she enjoyed having me to talk to because I listened. She spoke candidly during our conversations, so developing strong trust did not take long. But despite this well-established trust we had built, the next ten weeks would not be without drama.

I was doing everything within my power to hold the adoption together. For two months, Jeff and I had our bags packed, ready to zip to Arkansas at a moment's notice. She would call repeatedly and say that she was going into labor, yet she refused to see a doctor. All I could do was listen and encourage her to take special care of herself. She would also periodically disappear for a week or two at a time. Over those ten weeks, she would move twice and be unreachable because her phone was disconnected. Every time she would disappear, our attorney reassured us that she'd resurface soon and return our phone calls. He was right, and she would eventually check in with us with an explanation as to where she was and why she had moved. As much as we respected her privacy, our concern was knowing she was physically safe and could care for herself.

The birth mother was due on Sunday, May 12, Mother's Day. Two days later, on the evening of May 14, she called to tell us to start driving to Arkansas because she was on her way to the hospital. We again drove to Peoria so that my mom could care for Sarah, and then we continued driving through the night. Our attorney's wife, who also served as his office manager, called at dawn to tell us the birth mother had safely delivered the baby. She then gave us the number to her hospital room because the birth mother wanted to share all the baby's details.

Lilo was born on May 15, 2002, at 2:24 a.m. in a hospital outside Little Rock, Arkansas. Because the birth mother had moved, this was not the hospital Jeff and I had toured a few months before. Neither the hospital social worker nor the nurses had much, if any, experience with adoption. As a result, they feared accidentally giving or asking for identifying information; therefore, no one was talking. The birth mother had made it abundantly clear to them that Jeff and I were the parents, so any questions or information regarding the baby was to be directed to us.

It was not an easy delivery, but at seven pounds, nine ounces, Lilo was blue-eyed and beautiful. Their skin was fair and flawless, and their hair was so blonde it was almost white and barely visible. They had a perfectly shaped head with tiny, delicate features. Lilo was so perfect; they looked more like a porcelain doll than a newborn! Six hours after the delivery, our baby was in my arms. All the disappointments and devastating miscarriages had been traumatic. Still, as I held our new baby, I recognized that we had to experience heartbreak in order to get to that moment. The entire experience was truly surreal.

When it came to placing Lilo with us, their birth mother was very sure of her decision. She considered herself our surrogate, and her maturity in the hospital was astounding. However, as confident as she was in her decision, it was extraordinarily difficult for her to remain in the hospital after the birth for fear of getting too attached to the baby. She chose to discharge herself early against the doctor's advice. We both shed a lot of tears when we said our goodbyes. There were, and still are, no words to convey our gratitude for such a miraculous gift.

The minute Lilo's birth mother left the hospital, the nurses bombarded us. They all just wanted to celebrate. They could not wait to share every detail of our baby's birth and to hear our story. The hallway outside our room, so quiet all day, was now bursting with energy. Jeff and I had not eaten and were completely sleep-deprived from our ten-hour trek to Little Rock. The nurses encouraged us to leave the hospital at 9:00 p.m. to grab a bite to eat and rest up because we'd be going home with our newborn the next day.

The next afternoon, Lilo was discharged into our care. However, before we could take our brand-new baby home, we had to abide by the laws of the State of Arkansas. At that time, we were required not to cross state lines for ten legal business days before our appearance in front of a judge. Once we appeared in court, the judge would issue a final adoption decree. We therefore ended up driving straight from Little Rock to Bella Vista, Arkansas.

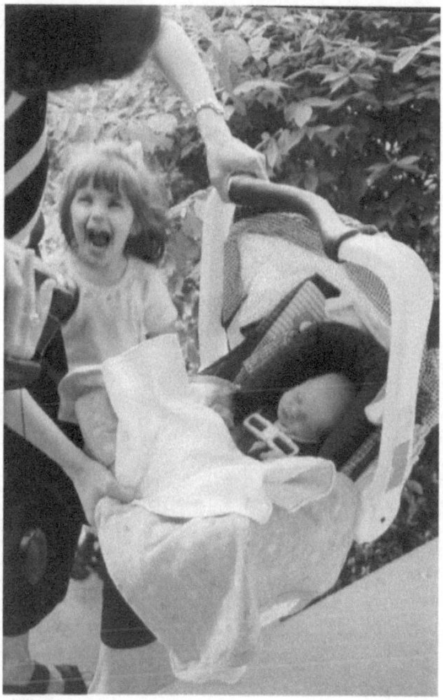

Big sister Sarah meets Lilo for the first time—May 29, 2002

We stayed in a two-bedroom condo in the northwest corner of Arkansas, close to the border. Jeff and I were anxious to leave the state and cross into Missouri to get Lilo home. (I could never have known then how ironic wanting to get into Missouri would become fifteen years later.) As luck would have it, our tenth legal day fell on the Saturday of Memorial Day weekend. Because the courts are not open on weekends or holidays, we needed to stay five additional days until we could meet in the judge's chambers on Wednesday, May 29, 2002.

The fear of something potentially going wrong with the adoption kept Jeff and me from telling almost anyone where we were or why we were there. Once our Final Decree of Adoption had been granted, we called Sarah from the courthouse to tell her we were coming home with her new baby sibling. I couldn't wait to call everyone else I knew, so I never put down my cell phone during the entire car ride. Our next month's bill with $500 worth of roaming charges proved it! We pulled into our driveway nine hours later, with my entire family standing on the porch waiting to meet our newest addition.

After Sarah's unexpected arrival and the struggle to adopt Lilo, we felt perfectly content with our family. However, Jeff and I hoped to add one more child to our mix. We were beginning the process of a second adoption when our greatest wish came true. In February 2004, months after moving my dad into assisted living after he

The Baurer family is complete: Sarah (6), Lilo (2½), and Brooke (3 mos.)—January 2005

was diagnosed with Alzheimer's, I learned I was pregnant again! On October 22, 2004, Brooke Elizabeth Baurer was born at 1:16 a.m. She came into this world as a belated—by just one hour and sixteen minutes—birthday gift to Jeff. While he claimed that I was late with his gift, he also said he should have known she'd be a girl because most daughters would never want to share a birthday with their dad. She was very definitely the icing on his birthday cake. She was also one day shy of her due date and an easy delivery. Most especially, she was the baby our doctors told us we "could never conceive and carry safely to term."

Chapter 4

LILO

Who am I? I am the kid with tired eyes and mysterious thoughts. I am the one who tried and tried until giving up on my dreams was easier than making them come true.

—LILO BAURER

When people ask me what my childhood was like, I explain that I grew up in a house full of joy and love. Being adopted, I always craved a sense of safety and security. For me, that feeling of safety was exemplified in my dad. When I was young, Dad traveled a lot. The nights he would return from a trip were always very exciting for my sisters and me because we missed him. Sarah and Brooke would greet him at the door, but I always wanted to be the first he hugged. Whenever he came through the door and yelled, "I'm home!" I would drop whatever I was doing and make a mad dash toward him, running as fast as my legs would carry me. I wouldn't stop running until my arms wrapped tightly around his torso. My dad used to call me "Lil' O," which quickly became Lilo.

I grew up with two seemingly perfect sisters, one older, Sarah, and one younger, Brooke. My parents' connection was the glue that held our family together. I can still see my dad taking my mom by the waist and dancing around our kitchen until she couldn't stop laughing. I could see in their eyes that they really loved each other. They had a love I've always admired and hope to have someday.

My parents frequently demonstrated their love for my sisters and me through acts of service. No matter what, we could count on them. Dad was always investing time and energy in our relationship. Most days, he would teach me something. My dad was the one who taught me how to ride a bike and helped patch up my knees when I fell. He also taught me how to play tennis. We would hit balls against the wall at the court for hours, laughing and enjoying being outside together.

But it wasn't just me whom he helped. My dad always had a fatherly influence on people. Everywhere he went, people loved him. I picked up on this at an early age when I saw how much the cashiers at Dunkin' Donuts appreciated him joking with them in Spanish on Sunday mornings after church. He was very kind and always thought of others.

More than anything, he loved to be involved in our lives. He loved when our school would have field day. He would go above and beyond as a parent volunteer and even let us paint his face however we wanted. Our classmates loved our dad as many of them had been coached by him over the years, most especially for Sarah's soccer and softball teams. Within our tight-knit community, he was known as a family man with a big, bubbly personality.

Growing up, my mom also played an active role in our lives. She was constantly volunteering at our schools. Even though I hated Girl Scouts, having my mom by my side as our troop leader was always fun. She helped me with school projects whenever I needed her. I struggled with math, and my mom was always willing to help me with my homework to ensure I wouldn't get too far behind. I knew my mom would be there for me if I ever needed something—anything at all. She has always been such a loving and caring parent. When I was in kindergarten, she would pick me up every Friday after school and take me to Applebee's for lunch. That was my favorite part of the week, and I always looked forward to it because she made me feel special.

I grew up with a passion for dance. I tried many sports, but I didn't enjoy any of them as much as I liked dancing. I started dancing at two years old, and it felt natural. Sarah had tried dance before me but chose to follow her passion for softball and basketball instead. She and I used to devise little dance routines to songs on a CD player and perform them for my parents. We were really close then. We found fun ways to be creative together. Sarah has always been very active, so we took long bike rides to nearby parks and climbed trees. High up in the canopies, we shared secrets and talked for hours.

When Brooke was old enough, she began taking dance classes with me. She played many different sports, such as soccer and basketball, but her love for dance grew each year. We loved going to dance practice, learning new movements, and hearing we were doing well or how much we were improving. I found ballet boring and preferred upbeat classes such as jazz and hip-hop. Brooke and I would have Sarah choreograph dances for us to perform. This was one of my favorite ways to spend time with them.

Summer was my favorite season because of all the time my family would spend with Aunt Marcia's family. Our two families would pack up our cars and drive to Long Lake, Wisconsin, to my dad's mom's lake house. We'd spend at least a week at Grammy's every summer. This was my favorite time of the year. The lake has always been a very special place to me.

My dad would take my sisters, cousins, and me out on the jet skis. We had a three-person inner tube that we'd tie to the speedboat and compete for who could hold on the longest. I can easily recall happy memories of my Uncle Clark and Dad competing to see who could get us to fall off first. Circling around, doing donuts in the water would make waves so big they would have to slow down when going over them. We called these "Harry Potter waves." They launched me into the air with a big smile and uncontrollable laughter. Tubing with my family has always been my absolute favorite activity because it brings back the innocence of my youth.

One night on the trip each year, my dad would drive us all out on the pontoon boat to a small island on the lake with a single house. We'd always go at night, which made it a bit eerie. The island he boated us to was called "Ghost Island." My dad would dramatically cut the engine at the right moment, shine a flashlight on his face, and tell us how the island got its mysterious name. He was such a good storyteller. We heard the same story every year, but somehow, he always managed to keep us on the edge of our seats.

Jeff and Lilo at Long Lake—August 2007

The lake was also special because it's where Brooke, my cousin Jeb, and I all had the freedom to roam the property. The three of us were inseparable. We played make-believe games, like pretending we were villagers in a town. We'd collect acorns and offer them to our moms in a concoction we called "acorn soup."

★ ★ ★

Thanks to the heavy lakefront snowfall, we had "white" Christmases most years. This was always a cherished holiday of the Baurers. One of my favorite quirky traditions is known in our family as "The Pickle," a game we would play on Christmas Eve. All the cousins who were twelve years old or younger lined up in my Nana's (my mom's mother's) room from youngest to oldest. The adults would hide a pickle-shaped ornament in the Christmas tree somewhere, and the first one to find it won a small prize. I only won one year, but I loved the good-natured competition with my sisters and cousins.

Christmas morning, all the cousins would line up, youngest to oldest, and our parents would tell us to come out. We would walk over in astonishment to the mountains of presents. Some years, our jaws would be on the floor, and they took pictures of our overjoyed expressions like they were paparazzi. We all would get one present that wasn't wrapped—our "Santa gift"—which was the biggest gift of them all. After presents, we'd all feast on my Aunt Anne's delicious breakfast casseroles. Sometimes on Christmas Eve or Christmas Day, we'd all split up into teams and go on scavenger hunts or play such games as Christmas Charades and Left Center Right.

Some years we would go ice skating with our extended family—usually my dad's sister's family. We rarely saw them because they lived in Connecticut, so these times were special for us. Aunt Kim was also an excellent figure skater, so we would beg her to show us some of her tricks at the local rink. I remember my dad also being a talented ice skater from growing up playing hockey. He'd playfully push Sarah, Brooke, and me around on chairs on the ice. We loved laughing and giggling as we skidded around on the frozen surface.

Looking back, I couldn't ask for a better family than the one I was given. Spending time with people who can laugh and have fun together is great. I am incredibly lucky to have had these experiences as a child. Clearly, my parents loved me, and I loved them, and there was no question who my "real" mom and dad were. But happy memories like these distracted me from the pain I often felt. Being adopted impacted me in many ways. I knew from a young age that I wasn't biologically related to my sisters. I was a blonde among brunettes. I sometimes felt sad that my mom had her two little girls and then me—an outsider.

Knowing that you aren't living with your biological family is tough. My parents told me they didn't know anything about my birth family. As a young kid, this wasn't easy to process, and I couldn't wrap my head around why someone wouldn't want to raise their child. The kids at school didn't understand what it was like, so I felt left out. Sometimes, it felt like everyone else was laughing at the same joke while I missed the punchline.

Celebrating the Fourth of July—2009

Feeling like a loner seemed natural, but it made me crave and wonder more about my biological family. Once, my cousin Meredith heard me crying on the stairs. When she asked me why, I told her it was because I missed my birth mother, which she immediately told Sarah. Sarah couldn't understand why I was sad that I didn't know my birth parents and was mad at me. She couldn't understand how it felt to grow up looking different from your family and knowing you have parents out there that gave you up for some unknown reason. Being non-biologically related created a division between my sisters and me. It wasn't until I was older that I learned that these spells of sadness went much deeper than just "feeling different."

There were also other glimpses of what was to come. Despite enjoying dance classes, wearing form-fitting leotards never felt right to me. When my mom would have me wear tights for nice dinners or musicals in Chicago, I felt very uncomfortable. Saying a prayer before each meal to thank God for our food seemed odd. Even as a little kid, I was skeptical of believing in God and Santa Claus. I never had as much interest in our church community as my family did. I'd rather have been running around the church with my friends. One day, I was playing tag and tried running down an aisle of church pews. While turning a sharp corner, I hit the side of one of them with my face and had to have a few stitches to repair the cut around my eye. I still have the bird-shaped scar all these years later.

Interestingly, I have always loved birds. I saw them as a symbol of freedom. I would watch them soar above me and feel jealous over their ability to fly as far as they wanted. Often, I wished I could just fly away from it all, away from everything that hurt.

As I grew older, the mysterious sadness in my personality seemed trapped inside me. I noticed that I was sadder than my classmates were at school, which became a difficult place for me. The only time I felt truly accepted was when I was writing. When left alone to express my thoughts on paper, I felt free. I loved creating my own mysteries from scratch. One ongoing story I wrote throughout elementary school titled "The Mysterious Man" was about a tall man in a black suit kidnapping kids who would never be seen again. The main character, the fifth-grade narrator of the story, was kidnapped and held in a warehouse. I provided details of feeling alone and attempting to escape, but when it came time to reveal the mysterious man, I'd always get writer's block. I could never identify him; thus, I couldn't settle on an ending.

Looking back, I wonder if my subconscious was actually writing about my birth father. Growing up, I knew nothing about my birth family. My birth dad was always a mystery I couldn't solve. In many ways, this man I've never met has always been a piece of my childhood.

With encouragement from several teachers over the years, I stuck with writing and kept improving—and my creativity and sense of identity started to take shape.

The Innocent Age

I remember when I would run outside without a care in the world,
I remember playing with the other little boys and little girls;
I was free as can be, laughing about,
Because I didn't know how my life would turn out

A couple years went by, was I innocent no more,
The new year gave me the key to unlock a new door;
The blue sky turned gray, the green grass became brown,
My eyes filled with sorrow, in which soon I would drown

The free bird that I used to be
Was now locked up in a cage,
My heart slowly filled with misery;
Never again would I see,
The Innocent Age.

(Fall 2015)

Chapter 5

LILO

November 25, 2012. I was ten years old. Brooke and I were sitting on our mother's bed, playing games on the iPad and watching TV. My Uncle Gregg, who was staying with us during his move from North Carolina to Colorado, yelled at us to come downstairs immediately. I remember his tone being harsher than usual. So Brooke and I ran down the stairs to find Uncle Gregg with a nervous look on his face. He told us to get our coats on because our dad had been hospitalized. We had to hurry because we were going to meet him. My gut had this feeling like my insides were tearing apart. I started to cry and asked him, "Is Daddy going to be okay?"

"Your dad is going to be fine; I promise," he replied, trying to give me peace of mind. I'm not sure why people make promises when they don't know whether they can keep them. We drove to a hospital twenty minutes away from home, into the emergency parking lot, right in front of the helicopter pad. Uncle Gregg told us to stay in the car. He locked the doors and headed inside.

I looked at Brooke with tears welling up in my eyes. "Brooke, I'm not trying to scare you, but I think something's really wrong. We are in the emergency area." She told me to stop. Things like this freaked her out. She was in complete denial. But my gut feeling knew better.

Sarah came outside in her softball uniform and hopped into the car's back seat with us.

"Is Dad okay?" I asked her.

"I don't know!" she aggressively responded, not looking me in the eye.

A few minutes later, a police officer banged on our window and told us to stay in the car. A helicopter would be landing right in front of us. Sure enough, a helicopter landed just then, shaking the car. It felt like a mini earthquake. A paramedic team pulled a gurney out from the back and wheeled it inside. Later, they came out with a person on the gurney, loaded him onto the helicopter, and flew away.

My mother, Uncle Gregg, Aunt Marilyn, Uncle Gary, and a nurse came out to the parking lot a few minutes later. Uncle Gary drove away in his car. Uncle Gregg got in his driver's seat, with my mom sitting on the passenger side. Marilyn was on the left in the back with Brooke on her lap, Sarah in the middle, and me on the right. The nurse opened my door to talk to us.

"Your dad has been moved by helicopter to a hospital with better care," she said.

"That was Daddy?" I asked her with innocent, painful eyes.

"That was Daddy," she reassured me. "He won't be able to talk to you, but if you talk to him, he will be able to hear you. He will be hooked up to different cords."

She kept talking, but my head was pounding so hard I couldn't hear her. My anxiety was so intense for a little ten-year-old. It was like in the movies when someone's thoughts drown out the outside world's noise. I watched the stars out the window as we drove to the next hospital. I can't remember how long the ride was. It felt like five minutes, but I think it was much longer. I remember how distinctly bright the stars were.

I remember praying to the brightest star I saw that my dad would be okay. "Starlight. Starbright. First star I see tonight. I wish I may, I wish I might, have the wish I wish tonight." I asked the star to save his life. He wasn't a bad man. I'm sure he'd made mistakes, but I needed him. My dad was my best friend.

When we reached the hospital, I remember it looking like a giant tower that could consume me. We met in the lobby, and the nurse behind the desk told us to take the elevators to the eighth floor. We got on the first elevator we saw, but it only had two floors. Floor 2 was the maternity ward, where life begins. We returned to the desk and a nice, blonde nurse took us through some hallways to the correct elevators. After getting to the eighth floor, where his room was, my mom went in to see him with Marilyn. Sarah, Brooke, and I sat on a bench in the hall. Papa (Dad's dad) came out of the elevator teary-eyed. I ran into his arms, and he hugged me.

Aunts, uncles, and cousins piled onto the eighth floor throughout the night. The number of people that cared for my father was never-ending. A new nurse came out to talk to my sisters and me. "You kids can go say your goodbyes. I'm sorry, but your father isn't going to make it."

The words I would never forget stabbed me so hard in my heart that I felt like I was dying too. I ran into my dad's room with Brooke and Sarah right beside me. A line of people crying by the wall in his hospital room watched as we hugged our father, who appeared to be sleeping. He had cords hooked up to him, and one was helping him breathe. I saw my mother crying for the first time in my ten years of life.

I laid my head on his chest and hugged lightly, afraid the hospital cords might become tangled. My tears poured onto his chest, leaving his hospital gown damp. I sat down in a chair beside him so Brooke could hug him. Sarah screamed, "Daddy! Daddy!" To this day, I can still hear her cries ringing in my mind.

I felt my stomach turn, ran to the waiting-room bathroom, and threw up. I started on a walk with my cousin Jenny down the hall, but then ran back and threw up a second time. I begged relatives to take me home because I didn't feel well. Before my aunt obliged that request for my sisters and me, my uncle asked if I wanted to say goodbye to my dad again with everyone out of the room. I said no. That is and always will be my biggest regret.

I left that night literally sick with grief, eyes swollen from tears, and a deep emptiness in my heart. I watched the stars as we drove away. I didn't wish on the stars that drive. I stared at them, full of sadness. They say stars can't shine without darkness. At that moment, I understood why. My dad died two days later from a brain aneurysm on November 27, 2012.

In the days that followed, our mom told us she was holding his hand the last few seconds he was alive. She said he squeezed her hand right before he passed away as if to give her his eternal love as he said goodbye. Her words were meant to be comforting, thinking that we might find peace knowing our dad was still out there, loving us forever. But for me, he was already gone; he died the night I said goodbye.

Sarah and I didn't go to school on Monday. When Mom asked us that evening when we would feel comfortable returning to school, Sarah wanted to go back the next day, craving a sense of normalcy. As a ten-year-old child coping with the first touch of major trauma, I didn't know what to do except follow my big sister's lead.

We returned to school on Tuesday. I sat in the back of the bus with the other fifth graders in a seat by myself and looked out the window. I remember being so lost in emotion that my thoughts were completely absent as my heavy eyes watched the world run by. Noah, a kid in my grade, asked me where I had been the day before. I turned around to face him and the other kids with tears welling in my eyes and said, "My dad died," and I started crying. The heaviness in my chest was too unbearable to stop crying.

Another kid was laughing from what he claimed was a conversation with his friend, but Noah thought he was laughing at me. "Dude, that's not funny. Stop laughing," Noah said, defending me, even though he'd always been mean to me growing up. Other kids who used to pick on me started supporting me because I'd lost my dad. My best friend's older sister, who had been unkind to me for years, said she was sorry for my loss. I remember her apology felt like pity. It wasn't comforting at all coming from someone who was so mean. Why were people who put me down before now so nice? My behavioral issues started emerging in my grief—a confusing yet eye-opening experience that shaped my identity.

Along with the dinners and sympathy cards, my mother also received a plaque with a quote, which she hung on her bathroom wall. When she wasn't around, I'd spend time rereading and memorizing the words because they comforted me. I recited them to my mom when I finally had them fully memorized. She knew I felt comforted because she ultimately gave me the plaque to hang above my bed. Every time I move, it's the first thing I unpack and hang on my wall. It reads:

> *Perhaps they are not the stars, but rather openings in heaven where the love of our lost ones shines down to let us know they are with us.*
>
> —ESKIMO PROVERB

My dad is my star, as I was one of his. I now see the stars not as something to believe in but as a reminder that they too come and go, and that's just the way of life. Taking a moment to stop and appreciate how the stars sparkle each night is my way of reminding myself that there are beautiful things in this world. I need to take them all in while I can. Stars, like people, die too.

Twinkling Bits of Hope

I like the way tears stream down my face. They are a mixture of coolness and wetness on my skin. I also like the sense of sadness that comes with them. I like the anger, grief, loss, loneliness, depression, pain, and especially sadness a single tear can carry, followed by many more, as it travels down my empty face. Once my face is cleansed by what I believe are the most powerful of emotions, then and only then, will it return to being calm. The kind of calm that washes over you like a waterfall that you drown in hits me in a wave. A wave so fast and fierce that it knocks me over so hard that the tears come streaming once again. It's a vicious cycle, kind of like a carousel that goes up and down and around over and over again until it stops. It's because I'm lost. Lost in my mind that becomes a growing jungle with vines of regret and misery. Lost in my head that's filled with voice after voice as they pile on more and more. I become scared. I become scared to live with myself when I can't figure out who I even am. Who am I? I am the kid with tired eyes and mysterious thoughts. I am the one who tried and tried until giving up on my dreams was easier than making them come true. Although this world is cruel and hateful, I have begun to accept what it could become. I have accepted its flaws as well as my own . . . I had a dream when I was younger that I'd live a happy life with my sisters and parents. See, what I didn't know is that wishing upon stars is what hopeful little kids believe in. I believed in the brightest star in the sky when I was ten years old one night. I wished my father would be okay as he lay dying in a hospital bed. The next day, he passed away and my heart sank. It sunk so deep into my chest that it split in two. My dad was the second piece of my heart. I like the way tears stream down my face because they sparkle like the stars I stopped believing in.

(Fall 2017)

Chapter 6

LILO

I always saw my dad as a hero. Looking back on the times we shared, I know I always will. He always lifted people up when they were down—even complete strangers. He played "Pretty, Pretty Princess" with my sisters and me. He once took me to a Chicago White Sox game. Although he was interested in the game, he didn't complain when I started falling asleep and asked to go home in the final innings. That's just who he was—willing to sacrifice for others. My dad made the world a better place for everyone who crossed his path. I am so thankful he adopted me and helped shape who I am.

One of my favorite days with my dad was his company's "Take Your Child to Work Day." My dad worked at Accenture in Chicago, and I got to visit the building where he worked and see his office. He made me feel truly special when he made sure to introduce me to all of his coworkers. When he finished working, he took me to the Billy Goat Tavern, one of the underground restaurants beneath the subway tracks. He ordered me two double cheeseburgers and a triple cheeseburger. I ate every single bite.

After my dad died, I lost my insatiable appetite, even with all the sympathy casseroles from family and friends. On the outside, our house looked normal to strangers passing by. But from the inside, it felt like there were iron bars on the windows, trapping us inside. While the world kept moving outside, we were stuck, like wax figures inside a diorama that was holding us hostage. Our den was silent now that my dad's audible breath wasn't there to fill the pauses between his fingers striking the keys on his work computer. It felt like my head was trapped under a thick, heavy blanket, and I couldn't see anything. Grief was all I could feel.

The feeling of loss is one of the hardest experiences to process because everyone grieves differently. Our society has many unmet expectations about how a person should mourn. People are expected to cry, but not too long or too much. Yet you don't care enough if you aren't crying in public or if you're having fun too soon after a loss. Kids at school made me feel terrible if I wasn't sad every single minute of the day, such as when a girl asked me why I wasn't crying and then told me she'd be crying all day if she'd lost her dad. We were all so young; no one my age could understand what it was like. Comments like these stung, and I never knew how to respond. School felt like a battlefield in fifth grade. And to make it worse, adults weren't much better. They expected me to feel sad and constantly tried to cheer me up, even when I was happy.

It was a difficult line to walk, and it was hard to navigate on many levels. I already felt different from the other kids at school, but these early, tough life lessons made me feel even worse. In many ways, I felt like how I was grieving for my father was wrong.

As my sisters processed the loss of our dad, they grieved behind closed doors. They kept mostly to themselves and kept their grief private. They weren't wrong to grieve this way; they did it in a way that made them feel safe. However, I grieved much differently. I was unable to control my emotions. My attitude and my mood worsened, and as a result, I was difficult to be around.

Our different methods of dealing with grief were an early divide that marked the beginning of my sisters and me drifting apart. We had never realized how our family of five had the seemingly perfect dynamic. Everyone was happy and felt connected. But without my dad, I felt a rift forming that divided our family, me on one side and my sisters on the other. The grief and the trauma of losing my dad at a young age triggered my depression and caused my anxiety to surface. My overall outlook on life felt more hopeless the older I became.

After a few months, it felt like Sarah and Brooke had moved on from grieving for our dad. I watched them go to sleepovers and spend time with their friends. I didn't hear them crying when I'd pass by their rooms late at night. Their happiness felt foreign to me because I still couldn't process the changes that had occurred. I struggled to feel normal while moving through my daily routine because it felt like the world was crumbling at my fingertips. However, like me, our mom also wore her emotions on her sleeves.

My mom and I struggled to fall back into our normal routines as quickly as Sarah and Brooke did. We'd hit an abrupt stop and had to rebuild ourselves over time. I would notice my mom not acting like herself, wearing a blank expression—the same one I wore on my face—and just spinning her wheels in survival mode because she was experiencing the crushing grief of losing her soulmate and best friend. Sometimes my mom or I would cry unexpectedly because the pain was always there.

My mom would agree that we both grieved similarly and grew closer through the grieving process. She would talk to my dad in the shower or before bed to feel closer to him. She encouraged me to talk to him in places when I was alone. I tried, but those places didn't make me feel connected to him, so I would go stargaze in the fields by my house and talk to him there. The stars were always there, and in their infiniteness, they kept my dad alive for me. I'd give him updates on how I was doing in school. I'd tell him about new friends I'd made or how Scarlett, our Maltese and Yorkshire terrier mix, missed playing with him. Other times, I would flashback to the night he died and have a panic attack. I'd think about how he'd never get to walk my sisters down the aisle or see any of us get married. The "what ifs" became overwhelming. My major anxiety disorder was in full swing.

A few months after my dad's death, I was talking with my friend Avery, who also had known my dad well. We were trading memories about my father. It felt like no amount of tears could fill the giant hole where he had been. We cried together, and I felt slightly less alone. She was the first person with whom I shared all the details of what I could remember from the night he died. As I told the story straight from my heart, shocked expressions consumed her face, yet she asked me to tell it again.

Memory is a funny thing. Whenever I would retell the story, the length changed. What happened was etched in my memory, yet details kept slipping out of my mind. I finally realized that I needed to write it down. I wanted to get the facts out of my head so they could be kept safe, unforgotten.

I started writing and found that it really helped. At first, I would write to my dad on his birthday or the anniversary of his passing, putting letters under his pillow for him to read. Many of the words just poured out of me. As I got older, I created a ritual where I would write my dad a letter to update him on what he had missed the past year. Then, I'd rip it up, drop the shreds of paper into a body of water, and watch them float away. Water and nature have always been ways I've connected with him because of all our family memories at Long Lake.

Nature makes me feel safe—as if my dad is giving me a pat on the back, telling me it'll all be okay and to keep going. He speaks to me through the whispering wind, the water, and especially through the twinkle of the stars. Nature's imagery is one of the best ways to describe situations and feelings metaphorically. I like that it can be interpreted the way the reader needs to interpret it. It doesn't have to make sense, but it should make you feel something. Nature is one of my muses; it makes me feel. I use my writing to create beauty from pain. When others read my poetry, I hope they feel comfort knowing they are not alone.

When I first began writing, it was a way to remember. Despite my best efforts, the memories of my dad fade more and more each year. I don't want to forget. By committing my memories to the written page, I've tried to preserve the times I shared with Jeffrey William Baurer, the man I knew as Dad. My mom and I have vastly different perspectives of the events that transpired, but we were both impacted by the void my father left behind.

That night has changed the course of my life in ways that have taken me years to process and understand. Losing my dad so suddenly impacted me deeply. Following his death, I stopped making promises, and more importantly, I stopped believing when other people made promises to me. My Uncle Gregg had promised me that my dad would be okay. At ten years old, I didn't know any better than to believe him. The betrayal shook me to my core when he unknowingly could not keep his promise. Today, I'm very careful about my promises because no one can keep every promise. It's better to say, "I will do my best."

After my dad died, I looked at the world differently than other kids my age did. An important aspect of my personality came from my grief: if I couldn't see something, I didn't believe in it. We held a memorial service for my dad at our church. He had already been cremated, so we displayed a big picture of him smiling in his comfy brown sweater. My mom keeps the same picture of him by her bedside.

People stood in line at the service, waiting to hug my mother. I remember feeling so numb and horrible. They were sobbing, hugging me, and telling me he was in a better place, but I couldn't cry with them. I felt so broken that my body couldn't process the stress. It was painful to imagine going through my life without my best friend. I had friends from my fifth-grade class there with their families. They were running around the church playing games. I played with them and my cousin Jeb until the service was almost over.

While everyone was crying and sharing memories of my dad in a separate room, I went to the altar where his picture was positioned, alone. Staring at his friendly, loving face, I could remember how his stubbly cheeks felt. I could hear his laughter as I stared at his dimpled smile. I could remember how loved I felt when he looked at me. I was feeling him so alive, yet I was staring at a picture. I talked to him for a couple minutes. I remember asking, "Why did you have to go, Daddy?" This is when I finally broke down sobbing. This is when the numbness ended. With each tear, I tried to reach out to him and cry on his shoulder, with his arms embracing me in his safety. But they never hugged me back. Now I can only remember his laugh if I focus hard enough.

Jeb walked up to me after I started crying and stood silently looking at the picture. Standing there with him in a "house of God," I felt far from everything my loved ones believed. I especially couldn't grasp how someone could believe in God when horrible things happen to good people. When my dad died, so did my faith.

During the first summer without my dad, my family and Aunt Marcia's family returned for a couple days to Grammy's cabin on Long Lake before continuing our vacation in northern Michigan. This summer of 2013 would be our family's last visit to the lake. While everyone was loading the cars before leaving to head north, I took the opportunity to go down to the dock. I sat on the edge, looking into the water. I told my dad I would miss him, loved him, and wouldn't forget him. Then, I leaned into the water and planted a kiss on the surface as if I were kissing my dad goodbye for another work trip. I didn't know it then, but I needed that kiss for closure.

Burning Waves

The water burns. I could tell you why, but then it would no longer burn. It would fall. Drown. He can't breathe anymore. The water burned him. I think of his laugh from time to time. His shaved beard slightly scratched my face when I'd hug him. His beard is no longer shaved, nor is it growing. He let me dance on his feet as he'd move to the beat of the music at the daddy-daughter dance every year. I could see the love in his eyes when he looked at me. His smile grew bigger and brighter every time I saw the edge of his lips curl. Now, whenever I see a helicopter, all I truly see is the one seven years ago when it took you to your deathbed. I hate seeing helicopters. I also hate eating ribs except on your anniversary because you promised me we'd have your ribs on that night. I wish I could go back to the lake where you grew up. I wish I could lay a final goodnight kiss upon your forehead as you did when you tucked me into bed at night. I touch the water at times so I can feel connected to you. You remind me that the water burns. Forever and always. You already drowned so I'll see you in the waves one day.

(November 2019)

Chapter 7

MARGARET

Without Jeff by my side, I was in shock. Hot, stinging tears were soon replaced with an icy all-over numbness. I felt like a zombie most days. While I was able to walk around and take care of my family, my mind was hidden far away, safe from processing the grief. His death was like being hit with a tidal wave of emotions I hadn't felt before. But as the months wore on and the stress of being a newly single parent mounted, my shock turned inward and became physical.

I spent two days immediately following Jeff's death hardly moving from the couch. My family was at the house helping with my kids. The kids wanted to go to school, and I was grateful they wanted to be with their friends and find some normalcy. After forty-eight hours, I actually stood up from the couch to pour them orange juice before they headed to school. Sarah looked at me with relief and quietly said, "Mom, I was afraid you might never get up again." This was the moment when I made an unspoken promise to my children. I was now the only parent they had left, and I would never let them worry about whether I would be available to care for them. I was determined to get up and stay vertical every single day.

The kids were very young when we lost Jeff, and our family was deeply ingrained in our community. Many felt the reverberations of our loss, but while my family was crumbling, I perceived that their "perfect families" and "perfect lives" continued. Our entire world suddenly stopped, and the one person who could help me navigate such devastation was the very person we were grieving.

Everything in my life felt like an orchestrated surprise attack; behind every corner, some new form of pain awaited me. What surprised me the most was how little we know about dealing with grief. As a society, finding someone who hasn't dealt with the pain of losing a loved one is impossible. Yet, no one seems to know what to say or how to interact when it actually happens.

I had individuals who did not even know me well offer their advice. The "you shoulds" became frustrating and very tiresome. "Margaret, *you should* meditate, listen to music, try yoga, and send your children to grief camp." I even had someone arrive at my door with a plate full of broken-hearted cookies. One parent of a friend of Sarah's told her that I was going to sell the house. Sarah came home sobbing, and it took hours to convince her I would not be selling our home. I had to sit down with all three of my children and assure them that if I were going to make any significant changes, they would be the first to know.

I was taught that when something is uncomfortable or awkward, silence can be powerful. Silence can work its way into the smallest spaces and fill them. However, people feel the need to talk during these crucial moments of silence. Society is afraid of being quiet for some reason—we need to fill the space. Unfortunately, I found well-meaning people asking very personal questions and saying much more inappropriate than helpful things.

What I appreciated the most were those who looked at me and said, "I have no idea what to say to you." I could reply honestly, "It's okay because when you ask me what I need, I can tell you I have absolutely no idea." I woke up each morning feeling it was necessary to wear a mask to appear in public. I wasn't sure who I might run into at the grocery store or Target and what might be said to me. I was never prepared for someone breaking down on my porch as I opened the door. I was finding myself comforting others rather than feeling comforted. People commented about how strong I was, so I did not allow myself to be anything else. Ten years ago, I had never heard that *it's okay not to be okay*. I hid behind my mask and tried to appear as together as possible. I was the only parent my children had left, so I only allowed myself to cry or fall apart for a few minutes in the shower or tucked away in the back of my bedroom closet. I had yet to feel how this illusion of strength would affect my physical health.

My pastor was perceptive enough to help explain the reason behind everyone's awkwardness around me. He told me, "Margaret, you are the poster child for everyone's greatest fear. It's not your responsibility to make *them* feel better. They look at you and think, 'What happened to her could just as easily happen to me. Margaret Baurer has to be okay because if she's not okay, then how will I survive this if it happens to me?'"

I did not find it helpful when someone said, "Call if you need anything." It then became my responsibility to determine *anything* they might be willing to do for me. What was much more powerful was when a friend would offer specific examples of how they were willing to help. "If you need someone to drive a carpool or pick up your groceries, please call me." These are the individuals we need when our life is flipped upside down—your true friends. But so often in life, we don't always know what we need until the moment we need it. There were unexpected things that would come up that I couldn't predict. I needed a person I could call at the spur of the moment. Minor inconveniences, like Brooke becoming sick while I was thirty miles away for an event with Sarah, quickly became single-parent catastrophes.

Looking back at this, I should have known that the months following Jeff's death were not ideal for starting new projects or taking on new responsibilities. But somehow I was persuaded to agree to an event that would become a massive undertaking. During the spring of 2013, Sean, one of Jeff's dear college friends, called me and offered to host a golf outing to honor his memory. It had already been suggested that the kids and I create a foundation and establish a scholarship at the high school, an idea that especially resonated with Sarah. A charitable golf outing would not only honor Jeff, but it could also help fund the scholarship in his name. Jeff loved the game of golf. He would head south every March with his dad and his dad's buddies to play golf for a week. I was anxious to celebrate Jeff's life with family and friends; a golf outing was a perfect way.

In the first few weeks, I was very excited. Sean had assured me that he had done this before and that it would be smooth sailing. He failed to mention how much I would need to do to pull off an event of this magnitude.

We set a September date to give us six months to plan so it wouldn't be stressful (or so I thought), and then we booked the venue. I immediately got to work. I had "save the date" cards printed, stamped, and mailed to family and friends the next week.

With the date set and as the weeks progressed, it became clear that the responsibility of planning this event fell squarely on my shoulders. I called Sean on several occasions in a panic. "Margaret, relax," and "It will all work out," were his refrains. As much as I appreciated his calm demeanor, his words did not secure sponsors or silent-auction items, create contests and games on many of the eighteen holes, track attendance, assign foursomes, or provide entertainment at the dinner. I confided in my financial advisor, who was instrumental in creating my foundation and scholarship. He made several key introductions and sat in on meetings with others who had successfully organized charitable golf outings. He connected me with the designer who would develop my website and design our logo. He negotiated Accenture's sponsorship of the event, and his financial firm generously sponsored a hole. He was extraordinarily helpful, and he graciously stayed behind the scenes.

My family also came to my aid. My sisters made centerpieces for all the tables, donated auction items, and brought many of their friends to the outing. My brother-in-law's company sponsored the dinner. Jeff's sister, Kim, also jumped in on the evening of the event to help check out all those making charitable purchases. In hindsight, I should have recruited my friends weeks earlier to help with the planning. However, Jeff had only been gone a few months, and it was difficult to ask for so much help. Therefore, I left no stone unturned and exhausted myself in the process.

Sean was invested financially, but I was promised active participation. To Sean's credit, this would not have been a big deal under normal circumstances. I had experience planning company picnics and holiday parties early in my life before starting a family, but after losing my husband and raising three young children on my own, I was more than overwhelmed.

I organized a binder complete with tabs labeling each section. I had contracts for the venue, DJ, and sponsors, and contacted printing companies to create the signage, banners, and special golf flags. In fact, this binder was very similar to the one I had created when planning my wedding. Only this time, there would be no honeymoon or "happily ever after" following the event. My late husband's name was attached to this outing, so there was no way I would allow it to be anything less than *awesome*.

Then life taught me a difficult lesson about how stress physically affects the body. Like all my siblings, I have always had naturally thick hair. That summer, while knee-deep in planning the golf outing, I went to a regularly scheduled hair appointment that changed my life. Seated in the salon chair, awaiting my cut and color, I was surprised when my stylist nonchalantly mentioned a thinning spot on the back of my head. I figured it was probably just due to the stress. Not worried, I told myself I'd be fine once I got through the golf outing. *I had absolutely no clue what was coming my way.*

A few weeks later at my next appointment, my stylist told me the bald spot was growing. At first, I ignored her observation and quickly forgot all about it. In August, a month before the event, I started seeing clumps of hair everywhere. It clung to the hairbrush like Velcro. It clogged the drain and littered the bathroom floor. Panic washed over me. I had very thick hair, which had (until now) concealed the hair loss. But when loose hair was dropping all around me, I could no longer avoid this unsettling truth.

Immediately, I returned to my hairstylist, searching for answers and guidance. Generally speaking, men face hair loss more commonly than women do. In many ways, gender is very performative. In my experience, this is especially true for women. A hairstyle is usually the first thing we describe to identify women. "She has long blonde hair" or "her brunette hair is short." I was dealing with profound grief, and I had not *felt* like myself since I'd lost Jeff. Without my hair—one of the most personal aspects of a woman's physical appearance—I would no longer *look* like myself.

My stylist had another client who was struggling with a similar issue, and she referred me to her dermatologist. When I made the appointment, I was optimistic, but when I heard the physician say, "Margaret, once it starts, there's no stopping it," my heart sank. I was devastated at the diagnosis of *alopecia*. I could barely keep moving forward. If it weren't for my three children and the golf outing, I might have had a complete mental breakdown in the physician's office.

Alopecia is an autoimmune disease, and my form of alopecia is usually brought on by trauma. Stress was the main trigger that caused my symptoms to progress so quickly. At first, I was concerned it might be connected to the autoimmune issues that affected my fertility, but I was told this was completely unrelated. I had no idea such a condition existed, and Jeff was no longer there to help me. Left with no other choice, I had to face the golf outing and still hold my head up high.

My mantra for that period was, "Just get through the golf outing, Margaret." I believe I willed my hair not to fall out quickly, at least until after the event. Each day, when I discovered more hair had dropped, my heart would pound, and my stress level would skyrocket. I knew I had to stay positive because my greatest fear was waking up one morning to find all my hair gone.

The golf outing was a huge success and truly a celebration of Jeff's life. I was completely overwhelmed by the number of family members and friends who'd attended. The highlight of the event was raising enough money to endow the Jeff Baurer Geneva High School Memorial Scholarship.

My instincts about making it through the golf outing were right. After the event was over, my hair began to dump. Within a couple of weeks, it had grown very thin, the texture had changed, and it no longer took hair color. My appearance was beginning to change. I was scared, and my children were very concerned. I had to convince my youngest that I was not hiding a cancer diagnosis from her. How would I ever find the courage to go out into public? Faced with this startling new reality, I had to prepare myself for losing it all.

My physician recommended treatment, and I made plans to purchase a wig. My mom was my greatest supporter and well aware of my condition. She knew of a wig shop in my hometown and promised to go with me. I drove to Peoria for the afternoon, hoping that hair extensions might be an option. The hair specialist, however, confirmed that extensions were not an option, as they would cause too much damage to my remaining hair. The entire experience of being fitted for a wig was harrowing, but my mom remained steadfast in her support and never left my side. Having shed many tears, I left the store with a customized wig that day, but truth be told, I believe it may have been harder on my mom than on me.

I drove straight back to Geneva following the purchase. Although I cried most of the drive home, I managed to call my stylist. Fortunately, she was incredibly understanding and helpful. She went above and beyond for me. She closed the shop and met me after hours that very evening. She was petrified to cut my wig, fearful of ruining it with a single stray cut.

Tears streaming down our cheeks, we decided it was best to cut slowly and conservatively. Each cut of the blade brought more tears, but we got through it together. It took us several hours, but she cut, shaped, and styled it close to my natural cut. I was beyond grateful because even though the wig didn't look exactly like "me," I could at least leave the house.

I was extraordinarily self-conscious and afraid that a sudden gust of wind might reveal my secret, but eventually, I adapted to this "new normal." Many people commented on my hair. Most of the comments were positive, stemming from the fact that they didn't know exactly why it looked different. I think a few close friends were suspicious but spared me the humiliation by asking no questions. Marcia struggled because she could no longer see the twin she had always known. It was also difficult for my children, but all three put on brave faces knowing I would not leave the house without it.

The entire first year without Jeff is a painful blur. I was living in a fog and functioning while in full survival mode. I felt like we were living in a fishbowl, with everyone watching to gauge how well we were coping. I considered my hair loss a sign of personal weakness. I felt guilty, wondering, had I sought help from a grief therapist sooner, could I have prevented my hair loss entirely?

Still, without him, we had survived all the "firsts"—kids' birthdays, our wedding anniversary, and all the holidays. It wasn't until the anniversary of his sudden death that it abruptly hit me: *I was truly alone.*

Jeff was gone.

★ ★ ★

Jeff always expressed his wishes to be an organ donor. Through the Gift of Hope organization, Jeff helped save the lives of more than fifty-eight people—an amazing legacy. Today, our license plates read some version of "Three Star" after the foundation I established in his name. The Jeffrey W. Baurer Three Star Family Foundation provides a scholarship to a graduating senior in our town's high school every year, which Sarah, Lilo, or Brooke awards at the Senior Awards Night in the spring. In this way, Jeff continues to give to others.

Chapter 8

LILO

I wanted to fly away from it all, away from everything that hurt.

—Lilo Baurer

I remember feeling disgusted when my mother held out a blue button-down shirt in front of me. It was a hand-me-down from a cousin that she actually thought I might want to wear. I was in sixth grade, and to my young mind, each tiny, white oval button looked like a mirror. The buttons reminded me that I wasn't "supposed" to wear a shirt like this. What I saw staring back at me in the reflection was a reminder that this clothing style was *for men.* I hated that shirt, and I made my mom donate it, after throwing a fit about keeping a "guy's" shirt. I couldn't wrap my head around wearing anything other than sparkles and flowers because in many ways, I was still supposed to be "Daddy's little girl." Sparkles have always brought me joy. They make me feel like I'm shining.

Gender norms were very strict in my mind at this age. Everywhere I looked, they were reinforced in my upbringing. At school, there were certain expectations around performing gender (the idea that a person's gender is just a performance made to please social expectations and not a true expression of the person's gender identity). After school, dance reinforced these same stereotypes. Even in the rare event when I went to church after my dad passed, I was told how to act based on my sex. Because of all these influences swirling around me, something as simple and innocent as a shirt with a collar and buttons on it made me feel uncomfortable. The strangest part is that it wasn't uncomfortable in a bad way, but in the back of my mind, I had this preconceived idea that I wasn't supposed to feel good wearing it.

Going into sixth grade was easier than the previous year in elementary school. All students in my district were now funneled into two middle schools. It felt good to not be known as "the kid with the dead dad" anymore. With so many kids at my new school, I could blend in more easily. But the anonymity made me feel like I was surrounded by strangers.

I was frustrated because it felt like I had to create a whole new sense of self overnight. My identity felt stripped from me when my dad passed, and I wasn't sure who I was supposed to be in the unsettling aftermath. I clung to familiar childhood comforts such as stars, letters to my dad, and bike rides. But now, moving into middle school meant I had to reinvent myself. In some ways, it felt like I had lost my dad again. Each time I progressed into a new grade, I felt his absence. He wouldn't see me grow up and become the person I was turning into. This stung.

When I needed it most, I met Bridget at school. Bridget had just moved to my town from Chicago. She had long, wavy brunette hair and smiled a lot. She seemed to fit right in to our small town from the first day she arrived. I had always struggled with people skills, and Bridget was a natural. I admired her for the confidence that just radiated from her presence. She was sweet and caring and freely gave her love to others.

Later that first week after her arrival, I was at my ballet dance class. I turned around, and to my surprise, Bridget was standing in the doorway. I was ecstatic because she quickly made dance fun. Having a friend to joke around with made me enjoy class much more. We had a couple classes together at school and quickly grew close. She lived in my neighborhood, so we sat together on the bus every day. We lived so close that we'd constantly bike or walk to each other's house.

She was my best friend. We knew each other inside and out. Her family became a second family to me, and vice versa. Bridget helped me break free from the heaviness in my chest, lift my head, and move forward with my life.

I also had another friend named Taylor, whom I'd met in choir class. She helped me to realize that I process trauma by using my creativity. I liked Taylor because she always saw the best in people. She saw my pain. And even though doing so was too much for others, Taylor stood by my side anyway. Taylor was the person I went to if I needed a pick-me-up. She could point out the positives in negative situations. She helped me express myself in many ways and will always be someone I look to when I need a reminder of strength.

We would turn our struggles into art, creating a special bond. Taylor and I would write and record songs for hours. We used our phones to create homemade movies. When that got boring, we would pretend we were disc jockeys hosting local radio programs (which was just a way to continue talking and singing for hours on end). Taylor and I would volunteer and sing the songs we wrote to residents in the local community center. We loved to perform and share our music. We went to choir camps in the summer and wrote and performed songs for our choir teachers. We also participated in numerous school plays and musicals together. Creativity was always at the center of our relationship. Taylor knew how to encourage everyone to be their best self, and I was no exception.

Around this time, Bridget befriended Evelyn, who had just moved from a nearby town. Bridget invited Evelyn and me for our first sleepover, and I asked if Taylor could tag along. That first sleepover was the start of our very special friend group.

Evelyn and I clicked instantly. We both struggled to deal with our emotions. Internally, my dad's death had triggered a mental health avalanche. She could relate to me on that level with her own depression. She knew what it was like to feel hopeless. She was the reason I didn't feel so alone. Evelyn created a safe space for me to be myself. I didn't know it then, but Evelyn brought out a more authentic side of me than any of my other friends could.

At our first sleepover, we did the most ridiculous things. One vivid and favorite memory of mine is when we each took selfies in the dark with our phones. We'd turn off all the lights and put our front cameras on ourselves with the flash on and contort our faces to take selfies with the most hideous expressions. That sleepover was the first time I had shared a deep belly laugh with anyone since my dad had died. We all embraced our weird sides and never judged each other for it. Bridget, Taylor, and Evelyn had never met my dad, but somehow they had become family to me. He would've loved all of them. They helped me feel accepted when I couldn't accept myself. In many ways, we were just normal teenagers. But then, without warning, life suddenly changed.

At the beginning of seventh grade, Brooke and I would attend Sarah's softball tournaments. We'd hang out all day in the park and choreograph dances with Izzy, the little sister of one of Sarah's teammates. It was clear to Brooke and me that Izzy was getting better training at her dance studio than we were in ours. She was better than both of us combined. My mother and Sarah saw this and convinced Brooke and me to attend a summer dance camp at Izzy's studio to receive better training. Brooke and I enjoyed the camp and subsequently switched to this new studio for our fall dance classes. Bridget switched studios with us too.

Unfortunately, this switch was extremely defeating for me. Everyone in my age group had been at this studio, learning more advanced techniques, since they were young. I was really behind and was now considered one of the worst dancers in the class. I had been one of the more advanced students at my former studio, where I was constantly praised; I loved dancing there. But after I switched, I never seemed to receive positive feedback. The competitive studio environment was extremely different. It felt very foreign to Bridget and me.

At the new studio, however, I did make a new best friend: Chloe. She was much more talented than I was and often received special parts in our recitals. Chloe really made an effort to get to know me and help me feel accepted when I was obviously behind. She would talk to me and genuinely wanted to get to know me as a person. That was just who Chloe was, and we grew very close that year. She always made sure our routines didn't make me feel left out. Whether she was aware of it or not, Chloe always made me feel included.

Sometimes at dance class, I'd feel hopeless the entire time. I was growing and maturing, so my body felt stiff and less flexible. I could not grasp new skills and pick up on choreography as quickly as Brooke could. I had to try a lot harder if I wanted to do well. My muscles ached as they were twisted and bent doing new dance stretches I'd never practiced. I couldn't rely on muscle memory like the other students could. Most days, I wasn't motivated to be there at all, wishing I could have stayed in bed and hide in my room all day, especially when Chloe wasn't there.

During one ballet class when I just wasn't feeling like me, my instructor asked me to correct a move. In that moment, I remember feeling so attacked over something very minor that I wanted to rush home to escape. I could feel the eyes of the other dancers staring at me in judgment. A chill of panic washed over me. My heart started beating faster in my chest as I could feel a fit of terror wash over me. I burst through the doors of the class into the sanctuary of the bathroom. I hyperventilated. I was stuck, hunched over in the corner of the tiny, one-person bathroom, until my mom came to pick me up. After this incident, whether it was school, dance, or home, I quickly started to fall into patterns of *cognitive distortions*.

I didn't understand it then, but I now know that cognitive distortions are negative beliefs about yourself that your mind twists to appear like reality. Many people with anxiety and depression can fall into these very convincing thought patterns. Thoughts such as "I'm not good enough," "I deserve the bad things that have happened to me," "I am a burden to others," or "I'm not worthy of love" can crowd a depressed person's mind. Sometimes we twist what others say because we don't believe we deserve the positive words we are receiving. For example, I might hear my mom say, "I love you," and my mind could twist that to "I want to love you because you're my child, and I should, but I don't, and I'm lying to you."

My negative self-beliefs were centered around me not feeling good enough or worthy of the time and space my life drew from this world. I started to think like this constantly. I was stuck behind a lens of depression, and I couldn't see life any other way. It would feel like

I had a rain cloud over me all the time, stuck in the perpetual storms that raged in my head.

Dance became nearly impossible to enjoy. School was harder to enjoy as well. During this time, Bridget, Taylor, Evelyn, and I would talk about our crushes at lunch and argue about which boys were the cutest. My friends were so sure of their sexualities, and I felt I had to make a point to be sure of mine as well. I often wanted love and affection because I couldn't provide any for myself. I would "date" a different boy every couple of weeks. They would make normal romantic gestures like hugging me or kissing me on the cheek, and I'd break up with them the next day because I felt uncomfortable. My friends said I was "boy crazy."

The uncomfortable feeling of hugging a guy or even just their physical touch was extremely frustrating. Throughout the day, I would have to stop myself from noticing what kinds of leggings girls at school would wear and how they looked. I especially found myself noticing my friend, Layla. I loved how she walked and how her face lit up when she laughed or was passionate about something. At first, I noticed a necklace she'd been wearing. But then, my eyes would notice where the shimmer of her pendant met the softness of her chest. When I realized I was staring at her, I'd blame it on being jealous of her appearance. I was *supposed to be into guys,* so jealousy was the only rational explanation.

At our sleepovers, Bridget, Taylor, Evelyn, and I would play Truth or Dare or similar games. As we were going through puberty and hormones were kicking in, we'd often sexualize the games. There was one sleepover where Bridget and Evelyn got dared to make out. Bridget's confidence created a space where she didn't care what she was dared to do; it was just normal for her. Evelyn usually went with the flow, while Taylor and I just watched it happen. Taylor was making faces like she was slightly uncomfortable with it. But I was unable to look away because I liked watching them kiss. I hated myself for liking it and couldn't comprehend how I, "a straight girl," could. After a few more rounds, Bridget dared Evelyn and me to kiss. It was nothing more than a second, but Evelyn was my first kiss on the lips, and I enjoyed it.

At school, I seemed to be an easy target for bullies. They called me names and criticized my appearance. My own denial and internal homophobia forced me to create a fake persona. The weight of trying to keep this other personality afloat was challenging. I wanted this fake persona to float to the surface, but I had to suppress my authentic self. It felt like trying to submerge a basketball underwater—while I was drowning.

Bridget and I sat next to each other in health class, and I vividly remember the day we discussed depression. Our teacher went over a slideshow of the symptoms, the warning signs, and what to do if we knew someone who was depressed. I remember thinking to myself, "that's me." Bridget looked at me. She must have read my mind because she knew exactly what I was thinking. For the first time, I realized I was depressed.

One day at Evelyn's house, when she and I were working on a creative project in the kitchen, her parents were screaming upstairs. Her younger brother got so scared by all the shouting that he ran away from home, and we had to frantically search the neighborhood for him. Eventually, we found him hiding in a nearby house that was still under construction. Evelyn's parents' fighting was a regular occurrence, and it seemed to embarrass her. I think the shame of their separation caused her to push us away.

Evelyn started making other friends at school and stopped hanging out with our friend group. She was struggling with her parents' divorce. I wanted to be there for her, but it was hard when it felt like she was pushing me away. Still, I fully understand why Evelyn was a safe person for me. She knew what it was like to feel completely broken. Evelyn's departure started to unravel our friend group.

I started experiencing more and more panic attacks and breakdowns in my classes. I was having trouble learning too, which made sitting through a full class period unbearable. When studying, I was frequently frustrated because the smallest noise or movement would distract me, causing me to lose my train of thought. My anxiety about what other people thought of me became overwhelming. But the worst part was I constantly found myself thinking about death.

I made a secret account on Instagram where I posted quotes that resonated with me about suicide, depression, and anxiety. Other accounts that posted similar content would follow me, and we would direct message back and forth. These strangers understood me and became my online friends. Weirdly, it made me feel less alone. I now had a safety net and a place to share my thoughts.

One day, while scrolling through Instagram, I saw a post that was different from any I'd ever seen. Someone had taken a very gory picture of their thigh cut open. The bloody blade was resting on their leg above the gash. At first, I was freaked out, but after a minute, I was still staring. Everyone I talked to on that account said self-harm made them feel better. I knew I wanted to try anything to make myself feel better. I was desperate.

I began by scratching my skin with my nails. I was too scared to actually draw blood for a long time. I had to gradually build up to that. Scratching became a nervous habit. I did it while in class, studying at home, and even at dance. It helped me focus when I felt anxious or couldn't sit still. My guidance counselor gave me fidget toys to use instead of my nails. But the toys didn't give me the same feeling of release.

As I became eager to hide my feelings, fearing other people's thoughts, I also became falsely confident. I was loud in choir class. I wanted people to hear and see me, so they wouldn't wonder whether anything was wrong. I would be obnoxious in the halls with my friends and wear a big smile as my disguise. Deep down, I wanted people to see me happy and not discover how bad my depression was. On the outside, I made sure everyone believed I was straight. I got called weird a lot for who I was. It took me a long time, but I finally learned that being weird is the best compliment you can ever receive. Even when their hurtful words stung, I reminded myself that I would never be boring.

As the scratching continued, Chloe started noticing my arm at dance practice. I told her the truth about what I was doing. I didn't have the heart to lie to her. She didn't know how to respond. Admittedly, I didn't know how to respond to my actions either. The scratching started as something I did once a week but soon became an everyday habit.

A few weeks after I saw that first post on Instagram, I found a screwdriver lying on a counter. I remember feeling drawn to the tool. I looked out the window to make sure my mom was still outside, and that I had privacy. Unthinkingly, I reached for this object that felt so compelling and dragged it along my skin. Because it wasn't sharp, it just left a scratch mark, so I pushed harder and felt more pain, but still no real cut. This was the first time I'd used something to hurt myself. This moment gave me such an adrenaline rush that I knew I had to try it again and cut just a little deeper. So began the downward spiral of self-harm behaviors and suicidal ideations.

After my family became aware of my self-harm, I was evaluated and accepted to a nearby partial hospitalization program (PHP). I was no longer safe without more supervision and additional mental health support. PHPs are outpatient mental health services; I wasn't admitted for an overnight stay. My school would send over my homework, and an instructor would provide me with the assignments. We had group therapy, individual therapy, and psychiatry sessions throughout the day.

I was terrified, but I quickly learned that this setting was safer than school. There weren't bullies to attack me for being myself. I didn't fall behind if I became distracted because the staff provided individualized guidance and were focused on helping me succeed. I felt accepted and no longer alone because my new "classmates" were struggling with similar thoughts and feelings. The teachers were also mental health professionals who were trained to meet our mental health needs. The schoolroom was ADHD friendly, with all types of swivel chairs and vibrant colors to stimulate our minds. Our therapy group sessions were usually raw and honest.

I favored art therapy. I remember one art therapy group session when our prompt was to draw a monster. Many students drew themselves, people they knew, or an actual monster like a three-eyed, furry creature. When we were done, the art therapist asked us, "Why is it a monster? What makes it a monster to you?" This session has always stuck with me because, ironically, I can't remember what I drew. I probably just doodled a furry monster with sharp teeth to complete the assignment. But, underneath, the real monster was taking shape.

While a participant in a PHP, each student is assigned a therapist to meet with daily. During one of my sessions, I explained to my therapist that I was hearing people in my head telling me to hurt myself. She helped me to identify these "people" as the various emotions I was feeling when experiencing a stressful or frightening situation. She revealed that she had another client who also felt the urge to self-injure. The client named that awful "voice" in her head Felicia, from the popular Internet meme, so that she could say, "Bye, Felicia," to push the voice out of her mind when it surfaced. I too ended up naming my depression "Felicia."

I drew Felicia to identify her in my head. Her appearance was the visual representation of feeling scared and broken. She had long, dark hair and was very pale. We shared a love for the color purple, which became the color of her shirt. The short sleeves exposed excessive cuts on her body, and the front read, "Wear long sleeves, or you'll look like me." I always felt she protected me, and that shirt foreshadowed my future.

Felicia told me stories that felt very real to me. She was the daughter of the devil, who had abandoned both Felicia and her mother. Felicia wanted to take her own life because of the pain of having no father figure. Her pain was my pain, so I felt like death was the only way to stop it. Felicia was so prevalent in my mind that I believed taking my own life was the only answer. Felicia was my monster.

Broken Promises

Broken Promises all over again. It won't be okay so stop telling me it will. The lies are getting in my head. She's engraving screams into my mind and I don't believe they will get out. It's so terribly loud. Drowning. Scratching. Breaking. Falling. I'm digging a grave of emotions and burying them too soon. Lungs are collapsing. Shattered. No air. Burning. It's all so fast. Too much. Please end. Please stop it all. Please stop breaking promises.

(Fall 2018)

Chapter 9

MARGARET

Every parent is told that the teenage years will be the toughest. Fortunately, I was kept insulated from this universal truth for years with our eldest, Sarah. She was a type-A high achiever. At the top of her class, I never had to lean on her too hard as a parent. But Lilo, as the middle child (four years younger), was the polar opposite. Naturally, I had blinders on when it came to certain, tougher aspects of raising teens.

As I look back on Sarah's high-school years, I may have been wearing rose-colored glasses. I naively assumed that the school system was great. In most ways it was, but from my perspective, only for equally *great* students. In our more-affluent community, tucked away from the harsh realities of lower-income ZIP codes, the schools weren't as equipped to handle struggling students. And that's precisely what Lilo was at this age.

With my husband gone, right when I needed him most, I had to learn to make do on my own. I could no longer divide and conquer like Jeff and I used to do when the kids were younger. My children depended on me, and only me. I had two other children who needed me too, but Lilo was demanding all my attention.

Losing Jeff was a total and complete shock. Similarly, Lilo's behavioral and mental health decline came on almost as suddenly. I had no forewarning that as Lilo entered middle school, I was about to jump onto the biggest roller-coaster ride of my life. No words can articulate just how much mental health impacts the whole family. We could not move forward as a unit because our family had to do so much work behind the scenes. The ups and downs and turbulence that marked this period in our family's lives were brutal. There's no other way to describe it, and I will not sugarcoat it. It was incredibly difficult and exhausting for all of us.

Jeff and I used to prophesize that Lilo would be our most challenging teenager. We even joked about how someday we would have our hands full. Lilo always marched to the beat of their own drum without hesitation—a quality we loved about them. They were our social butterfly, who knew no strangers and was not the least bit intimidated to confront or test authority. Little did we know that our once humorous prophecy would come true.

Before Jeff died, Lilo was a magnet to friends. Sadly, they never recognized this trait in themself. They were a natural leader in the classroom who was outspoken yet respectful. They excluded no one and not only supported but also protected the quietest students. Everyone in our social circle commented about how deep and perceptive Lilo was, and they would call Lilo "a little old soul."

Even as a toddler, they would ask the most thought-provoking questions. Lilo challenged me from the moment they began to speak. They asked me questions so complex and thought-provoking that I nearly drove the car off the road as they sat behind me in their car seat. Their questions were geared toward explaining an intangible emotion or about the thoughts and feelings of others. They often asked about our universe, the stars, and the afterlife. Lilo also wanted to know *who* and *why* certain words in our English language had been assigned to everyday objects in our world.

Just before enrolling in kindergarten, Lilo looked at me and said, "I don't think I'm going to be ready for kindergarten. I feel different." Jeff and I both agreed that a therapist might be very helpful to them. We knew that having an adopted child meant that there would be a lot to process. They saw a therapist for several weeks that summer. Just before school started, we could see that their confidence had been restored, and their therapist assured us that Lilo knew they were unconditionally loved and was very secure with their connection to our family. However, these initial concerns were just the tip of the mental health iceberg.

Lilo was a wonderful friend from the start, and fiercely loyal. They did not care if their choices were not popular with their peers. Lilo had a neighborhood friend who was also in their classroom at school. Their other classmates tended to avoid this child. She was delayed both academically and with speech, and often sat alone in the cafeteria and ate her lunch in solitude. Lilo decided to start sitting with her every day at lunch. Sarah, their watchful big sister, suggested to Lilo that Lilo continue to eat with all of Lilo's friends instead of isolating themself with just one student. Lilo, without blinking an eye, replied, "I can't think of anything crueler than to let a child sit alone in a cafeteria." My child has always been a champion for the underdog—befriending the quiet or less popular child, who had few to no friends to be on their team.

Lilo was heading into middle school for sixth grade. Sarah, who had been their protector, was now at a different building in high school. Brooke was still at the elementary school, so Lilo was now in a building without the comfort of a sibling. As a family, we were coming up on the first anniversary of Jeff's death. After the golf outing and losing my hair, Lilo and I both realized we needed professional help. I had been in survival mode for almost a year and was emerging from the *fog*. At first, I thought I could white-knuckle the grief. Family, friends, and my pastor were enough in the early stages, but Lilo and I needed more as the pain wore on.

Therapy was my awakening that grief is definitely a marathon and not a sprint. I wanted and needed a sprint after Jeff's death, but instead, I was headed for a very long road. I took Lilo to see Priscilla Brinkman, LCSW, FT, for grief counseling. Not only is Priscilla a licensed clinical social worker (LCSW), but she is also certified as a fellow in thanatology (FT). The Association for Death Education and Counseling (ADEC) defines an FT as *an advanced-level certification for professionals in the field of death and dying*. With less than a few thousand certified FTs nationwide, I was astonished to find someone with this coveted distinction in our own backyard. As much as her credentials and experience working with adolescents were impressive, what would become far more remarkable was her ability to recognize my child's behavior as signs or *tendencies* of significant mental health issues. At this early stage in our journey, I thought I would be devastated with a common ADHD diagnosis. *I wish it could have been this simple.*

In the spring of 2015, Lilo attended a presentation at school about depression. After learning about the symptoms, Lilo turned to their best friend and said, "I think this is me." Lilo then began to question Priscilla as to whether they may be depressed, an idea I immediately rejected. Priscilla worked hard to open my eyes to the very real possibility that my child was grappling with depression. How could my once energetic and enthusiastic child with such a zest for life be struggling? I thought I was doing everything possible to provide stability and normalcy in our home. If my child was depressed, what was I doing wrong? What more could I do to make things better? With Jeff's death came so much unsolicited advice, thoughts, and opinions from friends and acquaintances. This fear of judgment was incapacitating for me. If my child was this unhappy, what would people have to say about my parenting?

Lilo completed psychological testing six months later, and the results were alarming. I had come to accept the possibility of an ADHD diagnosis because of their lack of organization and inability to focus. I never expected high anxiety with a major depressive disorder.

By eighth grade, we were inching closer to the very top of the hill of our emotional roller coaster. There was no doubt in my mind that if we reached the top, we would plummet. Lilo's medication did not seem to be helping with their depressive symptoms. They became uncomfortable in class with their peers and would request a pass to go down to the social worker's office to decompress. It seemed that every interaction with a classmate, whether positive or negative, caused Lilo anxiety. I felt excusing them from class was important in extreme cases, but as they got more comfortable leaving class, the trips to the social worker multiplied. Inside the safety of that office, Lilo played games, journaled, or listened to music. Some days, they would spend the entire day there, avoiding class entirely. They'd miss the assignment and the lecture for one day, and the next day would be behind. Upon their return to class, they were quickly overwhelmed by the lessons they had missed. At the first sign of distress, Lilo marched back to the social worker's office, and this vicious cycle started again. By the spring, the vast majority of their time was spent avoiding class, so I could not imagine how they would ever survive high school.

I was very involved in my children's elementary school, but there were far fewer opportunities for parents to become involved at the middle-school level. Therefore, I had not established the relationships with teachers or staff I had become accustomed to during Lilo's elementary years. I would plead with staff over the phone to encourage my child to return to class. Every time I got Lilo caught up with their work, they seemed to sabotage it all over again. I felt powerless to stop their endless trips to the social worker's office. Lilo was either a snail or a cheetah. They were either behind, moving at a glacial pace, or moving at the speed of light. There was no in-between, no happy medium. Lilo loved to live in the extremes.

I admit that I became very angry during this period, though not as outwardly angry as I was on the inside. It took a tremendous amount of therapy to realize and understand that I was not nearly as angry at my child as I was with their behaviors. Lilo's troublesome behavior seemed to be a personal attack against me. Couldn't they see that I was paralyzed with grief? Didn't they know that every morning when I opened my eyes, I had to battle for every ounce of energy just to get out of bed? Some of the behavior I tried to rationalize as "normal" preteen drama. Lilo was obsessed with social media, but from what I could tell, so were all the other teens I knew. Lilo's phone became their sanctuary, and every poor choice they made appeared to be centered around something that they had seen posted. All I wanted was to get the phone out of Lilo's hands, but Lilo believed their phone was their only connection to their peers. I felt Lilo needed to learn that there were natural consequences for their actions, but their counselor and psychiatrist agreed that taking away the phone could do more harm than good. Lilo threatened me with their own safety if I enforced consequences. I was in an impossible predicament. I was defenseless, isolated, and living with the indescribable fear of losing my child.

There are no procedures or "how to" books on navigating or managing mental health and extreme behavior. There is no one way or "right way" to treat a struggling adolescent. Therefore, I began to call into question every parental decision I was making, as each one seemed to come at extreme risk. Lilo grappled with passive suicidal ideation, meaning they did not want to live, but had no plan to end their life either. Did I dare drive a carpool for Brooke's competitive dance and leave Lilo alone for even a few minutes? And whenever I did choose to drive a carpool, Brooke would jump into the car and immediately question Lilo's whereabouts and safety. I would assure Brooke that Lilo was at home doing homework. The truth was, as I pulled into our driveway, I would look up to Lilo's bedroom window and quickly say a silent prayer that I please find them studying in their room just as I had left them and not just provided them with an opportunity to end their life. There were days I was so exhausted and distraught that I let Lilo bend the rules just to keep the peace.

The first time I learned that Lilo was hurting themself was in the spring of eighth grade, and I didn't know what to think or feel. I was struck by panic, fear, and pain all at once. I wanted to take away their hurt and shelter them from whatever was causing them so much misery. I had heard whispers about an acquaintance's daughter who was cutting. My logical mind could not wrap my head around such an idea. Yet, a few months later, my child shared that they were hurting themself with a screwdriver and their fingernails. *I was beyond crushed.*

Self-harm is always serious, but Lilo's injuries were only superficial in the beginning. At this point, I felt Lilo was reluctant to significantly injure themself, which is the only reason I could close my eyes at night. Granted, this was not a thought I *ever* wanted to consider as a mother. Although their injuries may not have been severe, it was becoming clear that their depression was. Lilo was beginning to isolate themself in their room. They would run from the house on foot or hop on their bicycle at the slightest disagreement or when things did not go their way. I cannot begin to count the number of times during the day or night I chased after Lilo down the street or circled our neighborhood in my car to find them. During this time of explosive outbursts and impulsive behavior, Priscilla suggested Lilo may be struggling with abandonment and attachment issues related to their adoption and Jeff's death. She also introduced me to the very real possibility that my child may be exhibiting *borderline personality disorder (BPD) tendencies*. Priscilla, whose expertise is with grief and loss, was the very first professional to recognize these behaviors in my child. Lilo was still a minor, so it was inappropriate to officially make a mental health diagnosis until they had reached eighteen and had made it through the turbulence of hormones.

With Priscilla as my guide, I began to read and research. There was no question that Lilo was impulsive, which is one of many symptoms of BPD. As I thought back to their toddler years, they had always made hasty decisions without considering the consequences. For as long as I could remember, Lilo continued to gradually test the waters to see just how far they could push. My fear wasn't that they would purposely end their life; I feared they would keep upping the ante until they accidentally self-harmed to the point of no return.

Things continued to progress until, eventually, Lilo required hospitalization for their suicidal urges. They entered their first PHP in March 2016. For two weeks, they spent six to seven hours every day attending intensive individual and group therapy sessions and learning coping strategies, all while trying to keep up with their schoolwork. The anticipation of the many dynamic changes that would take place in my household was just the trigger to bring back my alopecia. Almost as rapidly as it had grown back, my hair started falling out again, one painful follicle at a time. I was *devastated* and forced to dig out my wig, which I had hidden away in the darkest depths of my closet.

Words cannot describe how ashamed I felt. I was desperately trying to hold my family together. Everything had been fine for a while, and my hair had returned completely. But I was now stuck in the middle of two extremes. All three of my kids were in the final year of their respective schools and would be transitioning to new ones in the fall. Sarah was approaching prom and high school graduation, thrilled that she would be attending the college of her choice. Lilo was participating in the last of their eighth-grade activities, and

Brooke was wrapping up fifth grade with a field day and picnic. I volunteered for many of the year-end celebrations, but the uncertainty of the upcoming summer was more than haunting me. I had to deal with the stress of caring for Lilo and navigating these intense psychological disturbances while celebrating all their accomplishments. I could not bring myself to even consider the anxiety Lilo was sure to face in high school. I was sitting on a seesaw. And to add insult to injury, I was doing it while wearing a wig.

I was self-conscious about everything. I was finally beginning to feel like we were no longer living in a fishbowl following Jeff's death. In some respects, maybe keeping my battle with alopecia private made it more difficult. I will never know for sure, but as Lilo's mental health struggle became increasingly more significant, so too became my need to control my narrative. I was mortified, and I could not bear the thought of any pity the knowledge of my condition was sure to bring. Several people had made comments, such as, "Margaret, I can't believe you're not pulling your hair out with all of this stress!" Little did they know.

Understanding what was involved in Lilo's PHP, including the many hours of intense therapy, I anticipated Lilo would be discouraged from self-harm. But it proved to only intensify things, and their behavior worsened. Lilo knew the vocabulary and key words to utter to a teacher, therapist, or guidance counselor: *suicidal, unsafe, self-harm.* These would force a psychological evaluation or "intake" assessment, which allowed them to leave school and reenter a PHP.

As much as I'd hoped Lilo's participation in a PHP would be the necessary wake-up call for them, it ended up becoming mine. As Lilo worked through their thoughts and feelings in therapy, they would leave shattered and highly dysregulated. I was then instructed not to leave them alone. With these few words, my shoulders tensed and my body became rigid. I knew I was facing yet another sleepless night as I would insist Lilo sleep in my room so I would be aware if they tried to get up in the middle of the night. I was also instructed to rid my home of sharp objects. It was crippling to know that any item in our house could be broken to create a weapon for self-injury. I removed all their leggings from their closet so as not to be tied around their neck. Everything with string, including the drawstrings in their athletic wear, needed to be discarded. Sarah, Brooke, and I walked on eggshells, terrified for the very worst.

Following a second PHP placement, Lilo continued to work with Priscilla, who became very aware of Lilo's fascination with being *inpatient.* She felt sure my child's behavior would escalate until an inpatient hospital placement became necessary. Priscilla tried to prepare me for this likelihood, and again, her instincts to do so proved valid. Within a few months, Lilo's continued and more serious self-injury resulted in a five-day inpatient stay at a nearby hospital. With Priscilla by my side, I was about to be thrust into a world I knew nothing about and found absolutely terrifying.

★ ★ ★

The first year following a loved one's death is often believed to be the most difficult—all the *firsts* without Jeff. Honestly, I remember very little of that first year. I was a robot. I walked around in a daze as I put on my "mask" to appear in public. I threw myself into creating a foundation, organizing a golf outing, and establishing a scholarship to honor him. My only goals were to secure my family's financial future and get my children to school every day. The next year, as the fog began to clear, reality set in that living without my husband while battling an autoimmune disease was my new normal. I had lost my husband and my hair, but I was *not* going to lose my child. I would do *anything* to keep them safe.

Chapter 10

LILO

The transition from middle school to high school was extremely overwhelming. It was jarring—like I had been riding full speed on the highway and someone suddenly slammed on the brakes. Like many freshmen, I felt lost in an ocean of strangers in an unfamiliar place. I was now at a much larger school crowded with new faces to memorize. Navigating new hallways to find my classes felt like being in a labyrinth. On the edges, watching me struggling, were hundreds of students silently judging me. Most of my time was preoccupied with overthinking what others thought. My anxiety ballooned until I felt like a ball of tension.

I was not ready for high school.

Evelyn was no longer in town. She'd moved out West with her mother and little brother. Her parents split in a nasty divorce, and we didn't stay in contact much afterward. Evelyn's departure left our friend group with a big hole that no prior bonding could fill. Taylor and I still had choir together, but Taylor was making new friends, and I could see we were growing apart. Bridget also started making other friends. Without my friends, I often felt lonely.

I tried out for my high school's dance team and made junior varsity. I was so excited because just making the team had been a challenge. My mom was thrilled and wanted this team to be the niche she hoped I would find. Like my experience at the studio, however, I felt the pressure and found the competition stressful. This team was not a good fit for me. Dance was still a passion, but I was slowly falling out of love with it.

In addition to dance and classes, I was experiencing puberty. I felt confused and disoriented. Everyone looked different, and there was a big gap between the eighteen-year-old seniors and a fourteen-year-old like me. I was at the very bottom of the food chain. Spanish class felt foreign—in more ways than one. Math classes were getting tougher, and I had more trouble understanding the material. I needed a math tutor to help me comprehend the more difficult equations.

In September, I went back to PHP for about a month. My habit of scratching myself in class continued. I had progressed beyond the screwdriver incident and convinced myself this was normal. My erratic behaviors became more noticeable, and I kept drifting further behind. In the outpatient program, I learned how to respond to kids who questioned my absence from school. Many of my peers would lie to their friends and say they had mono or a family emergency. I could never figure out what felt right to tell people, so I just told them the truth. I was out sick because of my mental health. My guidance counselor and teachers worked with me to make the transition back to the classroom easier.

I felt like a dandelion in a field of roses. Other classmates constantly asked where I was, and I found it embarrassing. I tried to catch up on the material I missed while at the same time feeling new to the school again because of the lengths of my absences. Nevertheless, I failed my Spanish class.

To help cope throughout the year, I assigned names and faces to specific feelings, as I had done with Felicia. After all, depression was not the only emotion I was feeling. My sadness was represented by Grieving Gretchen. I imagined her as a raindrop with a teardrop falling from her eye. When I self-injured, I visualized Angry Adam, a blood-spattered knife. Silly Sally, a purple crayon, embodied my creative and fun-loving side. Assigning names and faces to my feelings helped me navigate my emotions' complexity.

★ ★ ★

In the fall and spring of every year, several schools in the area offered the opportunity for their students to attend a weekend retreat facilitated by Operation Snowball. This international youth program spreads awareness regarding drug and alcohol abuse and mental health issues. Sarah had attended as a high-school student and convinced me to give it a shot. I participated in both the fall and spring retreats during my freshman year. The retreat was a safe and comfortable place to open up to others. It offered many activities that encouraged honest conversations and interactions. My favorite was called "Warm Fuzzies," where we each would tie a large ball of yarn around our neck like a necklace. We would then pull off a piece of the yarn and tie it to someone else's necklace while telling them something we loved about them—a warm fuzzy. Warm fuzzies had to be a compliment that could not be based on physical appearance. This experience stuck with me, and I have continued this practice by writing kind notes and complimenting people often. I enjoy making others smile.

My depression became a topic of discussion in my Snowball small group. My vulnerability encouraged another student to open up about her mental health struggles. She thanked me for making a comfortable space for her to speak poignantly about her difficulties, and she went to therapy afterward. This moment was truly meaningful for me, and I wondered if my mental health challenges might actually have a worthwhile purpose. This was the first time I'd realized that my experiences might possibly help someone else. Snowball was my safe place. I still have a warm fuzzy tied to one of my bags. After the retreat, I assigned my feelings of happiness to "Snowball," and of course, I saw him as a smiling ball of snowflakes.

Although my relationships were very positive at Operation Snowball, at school they were just the opposite. As I continued to drift away from Bridget and Taylor, I gravitated toward friends who could only be characterized as toxic. Two of them were Grace and Helen. They had very loud, outgoing personalities, which I admired. They were what my therapist would call "attention-seeking," but their confidence made me want to know them. People saw them. I desperately wanted to be seen too. And so, we became fast friends.

I didn't know it before I befriended them, but Grace and Helen were involved in a lot of drama. I immediately got sucked into their chaos. They got into many physical altercations, which kept me on my toes. Explaining why I leaned toward unhealthy relationships is difficult. But, at the time, they were a welcome distraction from the harmful thoughts circling in my head. In a way, their drama kept me safe from me.

I chose to leave my school dance team following football season. With tears in my eyes, I stood before the team during practice and explained that I could no longer continue. It was a sad day and a demoralizing blow, but it needed to be done. Thinking about the competition season was dreadful. Everyone on the team was fighting hard to earn their spot, and I was so depressed that any general correction felt like a slam. I couldn't handle the stress anymore and wanted to focus on finding a will to live. Quitting the team was one of the better decisions I made that year.

By mid-December, I found getting out of bed every morning an extreme challenge. My mom became my alarm clock when I wouldn't get up. I dreaded school, and I hated myself more and more each day. I had urges to self-harm daily. I wanted to know what dying felt like. On one occasion, I tied a string around my neck and attached it to my doorknob. I suffocated myself for a minute and then abruptly stopped. The pressure in my head was extreme, and it felt like I was going to burst. I couldn't hear anything except a ringing sound. Afterward, my mother saw the lines around my neck turning purplish-red. She immediately drove me to the hospital. This hospital visit resulted in my first inpatient hospitalization. It was December 2016, and I was about to experience lockdown for the first time.

Inpatient hospitalization is the real deal. It's not a walk in the park. It is for people who need serious, committed help. It is usually for crisis situations and is meant to stabilize you quickly. You are there 24/7. Once you've checked in, there's no leaving, and you're seen by a psychiatrist and therapist. Based on your assigned therapist's recommendation, you may be sent back home, to an outpatient program, or to a long-term residential treatment facility for further treatment.

While there, I had to wear clothes with no drawstrings and specific underwear. Every clothing item is scrutinized because the goal is to keep you safe. Inside wasn't bleak and sterile, with clinicians in white lab coats like in the movies. They wore business-casual attire and sometimes scrubs. There are mandatory group therapy sessions at various times throughout the day. They also had art and music therapy groups, similar to outpatient. My roommate was super kind, which was a good thing. Our door always had to be open. We were constantly being watched either by camera or by dedicated staff.

During one of our nightly dinners, a girl told us she was being sent back to residential. The other kids all listened in horror as she explained what it was like. Residential treatment is like inpatient for an indefinite period. It feels like a prison in many ways. The kids around the table were peppering her with questions as she explained she was a veteran, having been sent there before. She made residential sound horrible, and hearing her secondhand experiences cemented in my mind a new fear: being institutionalized long term.

I spent five days in inpatient before transitioning to my third stint in outpatient treatment. Because of the holiday break, I did not return to school until the beginning of the second semester of my freshman year. I had new classes and made two more friends: Tori and Mara. Mara and I connected because she struggled with mental health. Tori was one of the few openly gay students in our grade. We spent a lot of time together.

Mara, Tori, and I often spent time smoking marijuana and drinking our parents' alcohol. They made me feel like I belonged again. Sometimes, we would talk about the guys at school, and Tori would try to convince me I was gay. I always said, "No way," and laughed it off. Grace also started hanging out with us, so my two friend groups merged. Mason, a boy from a nearby school, joined our group about the same time. He was very tall and muscular. He was blonde and blue-eyed and had an amazing singing voice. I always thought I had a crush on him.

Grace and Mara lived in the same neighborhood, and we liked having sleepovers at Mara's. One evening after her parents were asleep, we snuck Mason through the basement window. We snuck out at 2:00 a.m. to buy some weed and get high. When an opportunity presented itself and friends were available to join me, I drank and smoked weed to mask my pain.

Once summer arrived, getting high with my friends and walking around after dark became easier. One night, Grace and I wanted to smoke at a park and stay out until morning. We had a small amount of weed, but we wanted more. Our dealer told us to meet him at a certain spot and wait for him. By 1:00 a.m., I was anxious because we were out past the town's curfew. I told Grace to carry our weed in her bra, but she insisted on keeping it with a homemade bong in her bag.

We saw the dealer talking to someone in a car down the street. He eventually walked toward us, but when he reached our block, he immediately turned in the opposite direction. Instantly, I knew something was wrong. The car sped forward. We could see flashing colored lights through the blinding headlights. We told the police officer we were going to Bridget's house and were fine walking, but he called our parents because we were out past curfew.

My mom came to get me from down the street, bleary-eyed from being woken up at 1:00 a.m. She was irate. She got out of the car, looked at me, and said, "What the hell were you thinking?!" She drove me home and told me I had to sleep in her room because she didn't trust me. When we stopped in the garage, she looked at me and repeated, "What the *hell* were you thinking?" in a tone that still makes me cringe.

I looked back at her and said calmly, "When will you get it? I don't want to be here. *I don't want to be alive.*"

My mom would later tell me this was the night she realized I was not okay.

Grace's parents and sister did not answer their phones, so the officer drove her to the police station, where they discovered her marijuana and paraphernalia. The police called again to tell my mom that Grace had marijuana but claimed that it belonged to me. Ultimately, Grace was the only one charged with possession.

The next morning following my curfew violation, I knew my mother was angry, but I had no idea what she was planning. In the middle of the afternoon, I was in my room coloring when several police officers entered. They escorted me from my home to the ambulance waiting outside. Involuntarily, I was once again on my way to the hospital and extremely angry at my mom.

I spent another week at the same facility as my first inpatient placement before being transported to Concordia Health—a residential treatment center in Indiana my assigned therapist had recommended. I was a resident there for two months that summer. There were roughly fifteen girls locked on the floor; some of us had roommates and others had private rooms.

When you would first arrive, you would be put on one-to-one supervision. A staff member had to be within six feet of you at all times—24/7. They would watch you shower and use the bathroom out of their peripheral vision to ensure you were safe. All our hygiene products were stored and locked. We had a strict schedule. We did our schoolwork, sent from our various high schools, with markers and crayons because their blunt tips couldn't be weaponized. When we were allowed outside, it was in a fenced area for a set interval. We weren't allowed to touch anyone. They'd record how much food we ate at meals. There were no alternative options to eat. Residential was extremely violating.

While I was there, I met Everett, who changed my life. Everett walked in on their first day with short blonde hair, glasses, and a blue short-sleeved button-up (just like the one my mom and I had thrown out all those years before). When they entered the room, they immediately made eye contact with me. We shared a brief but intense smile.

During the evenings, when we had free time, Everett and I would sit at the tables talking and learning about each other. Sometimes we'd play ukulele together, or they'd play their guitar. They had an angelic voice. It comforted me. Everett and I would secretly hold hands or touch each other's thighs under the tables because it was out of sight from cameras. I consider them my first love. They made me finally realize and accept that I am gay. When my mom, Sarah, and Brooke visited, I came out to them as bisexual. My mother looked at me and said, "Stop trying to put on a show." That was the first time in my life that my mom didn't accept me.

I left Concordia Health a couple weeks before Everett was discharged. I was allowed to give everyone hugs before leaving, and Everett and I cried a lot when I said goodbye. They told me they loved me quietly as we embraced one last time and snuck our contact information to each other. This wasn't allowed because you weren't supposed to know anyone after you left. We had an "on again, off again" long-distance relationship that was very unhealthy for a few years afterward.

Many friends I made at Snowball attended a nearby Catholic school. Before my sophomore year, my mother decided to pull me from my public high school and enroll me there, thinking I would get the help and support I needed from the smaller class sizes. This school was very strict, requiring me to wear a uniform and pray. I was not religious and didn't like being forced to wear a skirt to school every day. I begged her repeatedly not to make me go.

I was at that school for just five days. On the fifth day, I went into the bathroom and cut myself using a pencil sharpener blade. The incision went all the way down my arms. I watched myself bleeding in the mirror, and as the blood ran down my arms, tears streamed down my face. I was suicidal and had just injured myself pretty badly. I knew the hell that awaited me if I left that bathroom. Another admission to the local hospital and more residential. I would be forced back into an institution.

I remember telling myself it would all feel better when it was over, as Felicia had told me. I held the blade to my neck, trying hard to cut it, but I couldn't. I didn't have the courage, and I ended up throwing my blade in the trash can. I walked down the hall with bleeding arms, leaving a trail of red behind me on the shiny white linoleum. I went to the guidance office, and a counselor called my mom, who rushed me to a nearby hospital.

I was hospitalized at a new inpatient facility for a week. While there, journaling and writing poetry made life much easier for me. I came out of this hospitalization with a sense of purpose for the first time since my dad had died. I was finally ready to try. And I truly believed my dad was with me.

First Love

And then you left me . . .
except you didn't really leave.
There's a string that you tied around
each vein running through my barely pulsing
heart. Even though we are miles apart you somehow
have a good grasp on the string. You pull and you pull
and I don't believe you even know how badly it hurts. It's
like you're a beautiful balloon I can't seem to let go of. And I
sometimes wish that when you left you had untied the string
that keeps me full of such desire to taste you, to hold you, to
live as one. But I can't figure out why it still feels like this.
After years of not looking into your eyes I still think your
beautiful parts are lingering within my soul. We are
stars away but maybe I'm just not letting the
string go. You are still pulling away but
the other end . . . I can't let it leave
my heart. I want to engrave
you into my veins.
Maybe there
is no
s
t
r
i
n
g

Maybe there's just me and my memories of you.
Maybe you've let me go and that's what truly hurts my heart.

(Spring 2019)

Chapter 11

MARGARET

Life has many moments—tender moments—when words seem to fail. Explaining to young adolescents why their sibling has been committed to a hospital to help keep them safe is one of them. At the time, I didn't have the vocabulary to adequately describe Lilo's behavior and to justify why I was forced into making such a harrowing decision. To the outside world, it was like they had just disappeared. When Lilo mysteriously vanished, dealing with the other parents was one thing, but explaining it to Brooke's inquisitive young friends was another. After multiple emotionally draining hospitalizations, our family desperately needed relief after Lilo's hellacious freshman year.

I am unsure how Brooke and I survived Lilo's first year in high school. There were several PHP and inpatient placements, followed by weeks of playing catch-up for all of the classes and schoolwork missed. Due to our proximity to the high school, when Lilo was in attendance, they would bring home a classmate every day. Not close friends, mind you, but peers whom I had never met—and someone new each afternoon. Lilo didn't always know them particularly well. They brought them home under the pretense of studying and then demanded they stay for dinner and into the evening. These kids always seemed available and were never expected to be home by any particular time. Brooke would walk in the door from school and instantly ask how many strangers were in our house. I have to admit that Lilo was the safest in the presence of a peer, and safety was exactly what was threatened when I insisted these kids must leave before dinner. Once again, I was losing all control of my house and my child. Brooke and I were losing our minds.

No one was more grateful than I was when Lilo's tumultuous freshman year finally ended. It was the first week of summer, and I had agreed to allow Lilo to spend the night at Bridget's house. It was to be only the two of them. I believed that Bridget's parents were on board, and I went to bed, hoping for a peaceful night's sleep. I woke up at 1:00 a.m. to an alarming banging on my front door and loud tapping on the first-floor windows. Our dog was barking uncontrollably. I ran down the stairs to find beams from flashlights shining through every window. My heart was pounding and my body trembling when I opened the door to find several police officers standing on my porch. "Are you the mother of Lilo Baurer?" were the only words I heard. At that moment, my body went numb. I immediately had a flashback to the very second I had become aware that I had lost my husband. "Oh my God, are they alright?" was all I could mutter. The officer responded that they're alright and just around the corner, and that Lilo and their friend had been ticketed for a curfew violation. My body was still trembling but no longer from fear. The only emotion I could now feel was absolute fury.

I had experienced many unexpected behaviors from my child, but until this moment, Lilo had never been dishonest. They had been at Bridget's house, but there was never going to be a sleepover. Lilo and Bridget had conjured up this sleepover plan to hide Lilo's real plan.

I had forbidden Lilo to hang out with one particular peer, someone who had proven over and over throughout her freshman year that she could not be trusted. The plan was for Lilo and this teen, Grace, to hang out together and roam around our town all night. The worst was that Lilo and Grace had been allowed to *walk* out of Bridget's house at midnight without my knowledge.

I jumped into my car and followed the officers around the corner to pick up my child. Lilo looked at me and, knowing I was furious, hopped into the back seat. After pulling into the garage, I turned off the ignition and closed the garage door. With a tone that cannot be described, I turned around, looked them directly in the eyes, and bellowed, "What in the hell were you thinking?!" What I heard them say next would change the trajectory of our path.

"When will you get it? I don't want to be here. I don't want to be alive."

These words were the wake-up call I needed. The next day, as my child behaved as if nothing had transpired the night before, I went to work on a new mission. Lilo was refusing treatment and had no intention of returning to the hospital. They had no interest in group therapy and planned to spend the entire summer doing as they wished. After making a plan for Sarah and Brooke to be away from home, it was with a huge lump in my throat and conflicting self-talk racing through my mind that I walked outside to call our local police department. I made arrangements for officers to come to our home and escort Lilo to the hospital. I asked them to arrive with no sirens, as I did not want Lilo to hear them and run.

While awaiting their arrival and struggling with guilt, I walked by Lilo's room. They were lying on the floor sketching on their favorite art pad. They looked like the sweet and innocent kindergartner they once were, surrounded by their favorite coloring books. Unfortunately, I knew in no time at all, this sweet child would again become a very angry and troubled teen. To my surprise, the officers parked their vehicles around the corner and walked up the sidewalk to the house. One officer stayed with me as three others went up the stairs to their room. With the officers inside, the paramedics drove up in an ambulance. I could instantly hear Lilo yelling. As they all descended the stairs, Lilo angrily yelled at me, "Is this what you've been planning all day?" While seated in our dining room, the police officer asked Lilo if they would prefer to leave the house the easy way or the hard way. They chose to walk freely to the ambulance, but only after shouting the most hateful words at me.

After a night in the ER, Lilo was transferred to another nearby hospital for inpatient care. Lilo was beyond irate, and I knew I had not much more than seventy-two hours before the facility would start discussing their release. I was there every day for either family therapy or visiting hours. Sarah and Brooke visited too. Lilo was too angry to participate in groups or activities with the other patients. I pleaded for a longer stay. I needed to buy time until I could find an appropriate therapeutic program for them.

Within the first couple days, Lilo's assigned therapist at the hospital agreed that a longer and more intensive program was needed. Having received some recommendations, I spent hours on the phone looking for an appropriate placement and an available bed. I was shocked to find so few programs, and what programs that did exist had very long waiting lists. After eight days at the hospital, Lilo was ultimately transferred to Concordia Health in Indiana for a six-week therapeutic residential program. After notification of their safe arrival, I closed my eyes and slept through the night for the first time in two years.

I spent every weekend that summer driving back and forth to Indiana. I participated in family therapy and completed all reading and written assignments. Sarah and Brooke were asked to attend a few sessions as well. The amount of work required from the entire family cannot be denied. By the first of August, Lilo returned home with a "family contract" in hand. This contract contained all the expectations for living in our home safely and the potential consequences of not honoring the contract. This document was something that all four of us had written and agreed to together, but what I didn't know was that Lilo had no intention of following it.

We struggled for the next couple weeks before Lilo was set to begin their sophomore year in high school. Transitioning home after missing the entire summer with their friends was difficult. I was hopeful for a new group therapy opportunity, which was less than successful. In a last-ditch effort to hold our now crumbling family together, I threw up what can only be called a Hail Mary. I sent Lilo to a much smaller Catholic school about twenty minutes from home. At the time, I believed the smaller enrollment, block schedule, and more individualized attention might be a better fit. Contrary to their opinion then, I didn't send Lilo to Catholic school as a punishment. It was quite the opposite.

They had made many friends at Operation Snowball during their freshman year. Many of these friends from the program attended their new school, and many of the Snowball facilitators were faculty members. I thought Lilo would be relieved to be in classes with their friends. Sadly, I couldn't have been more wrong.

On the fifth day of school, I dropped Lilo off at the front entrance. Once again, I had to encourage them to get out of my car, something I had been doing all week. When they turned around to look at me before walking through the front doors, the look on their face sent chills down my spine. Something was not right. Instead of leaving, I circled the school parking lot for over an hour. An unshakable feeling in my gut told me not to leave the school that day. Chalk it up to a mother's intuition or paranoia, but I was determined to ensure Lilo was safe. My fingers punched the office numbers into my cell phone multiple times while I waited in pure dread. I called the office repeatedly, asking to be reassured that Lilo had safely made it into their first-period class. They couldn't reassure me because they couldn't find them. My fears did come true that day. Moments later I got the call that every parent fears. Lilo had self-harmed in the bathroom and was now sitting in the counselor's office.

I was in panic mode as I rushed them to the hospital. I was becoming too accustomed to the procedures that would occur once they were in the ER. Lilo's room would be stripped of everything. All counters would be bare, and the only things visible would be the hospital bed, the TV mounted on the wall, and one very uncomfortable chair. They would be placed on a "suicide watch," so an officer would sit outside the door. In the hallway next to the officer, my belongings, including my purse and cell phone, would be sitting on the floor whenever I visited.

My head, neck, and shoulders were tense from stress as I watched the drama play out like it had so many times before. My emotions raged. I was livid. My child had cut themself so they would not have to stay at school that day. While I was sitting on nothing more than a metal folding chair, Lilo was perfectly content in a comfortable bed with a food menu in one hand and the remote control in the other. They smiled at me as if they had just checked into a penthouse suite at a luxury resort.

I'm not proud to admit it, but as the hospital staff brought them warm blankets and dessert, I couldn't take it any longer. I had no intention of calling my sisters or Priscilla, who would undoubtedly offer to sit with me, as they had done during many other hospitalizations. I was starving and freezing in the ER, and I'd had enough. Nurses came in and out every few minutes, and a guard stood sentinel outside the door at all times. I knew it would take twelve to fourteen hours before there was an available bed at a nearby suburban hospital for yet another inpatient stay. I also knew that I would have to drive by myself late at night or into the wee hours of the morning to that new placement to admit Lilo. The stress of every hospitalization had compounded internally, and I needed to go home. Every moment I sat there, I felt increasingly judged. My internal perception of myself was that everyone was asking themselves what this parent was doing to make this child want to kill themself.

After this incident, I knew that I could no longer ensure Lilo's safety in our home. I couldn't be there to circle the parking lot until the school checked in with me every day to let me know they were alright. I was a single mother, and I had two other kids to take care of as well. It was time to look into a more long-term solution to help keep Lilo safe. Lilo and I had discussed that if a residential placement were ever necessary, we could research and choose a place together. However, they were now back in an inpatient program, and I had to move quickly to find an appropriate placement. I reached out to Priscilla, and we began seriously exploring options. We landed on one residential treatment program that stood out head and shoulders above the others. This facility was well regarded at the time. But I didn't take it at face value. I wasn't the type of parent who haphazardly sent my child just anywhere. I wanted to *know* that Lilo would receive the care they desperately needed. I talked to the directors. I researched. I interviewed other parents who sang their praises. I vetted it. *A lot.*

I liked this facility's approach because it catered to adopted teens. A vast majority of their population were adoptees. The fact that we still didn't have an *official* diagnosis for Lilo, coupled with the attachment issues related to their adoption and losing both of their birth parents, not to mention losing Jeff, gave me hope that this facility might be the answer to my prayers. I had done enough research to suspect that Lilo would relate and connect with the other adolescents in the program. I hoped it would be a place where they would feel welcomed and accepted. For the first time in their young life, Lilo would be surrounded by others who had also been adopted.

I assumed the other students came from loving families, similar to our own. Of course, some did, but unfortunately, many came from horrific situations. Some were foster children who had been abused, and others had become wards of the state. The simple fact was that many of the teens were seriously struggling and highly dysregulated. My child was walking into a lion's den, and I had no possible way of knowing. In hindsight, it was like watching a scene in a suspense movie, when someone decides to walk into a dark house alone at night. But I'm getting ahead of myself. First, Lilo had to get accepted into the program.

The application process for getting a child into residential treatment was more grueling than the requirements for applying to an Ivy League college or university. There are countless questions—questions about everything you could ever want to know about a child and their family. I was pulling all-nighters to accurately document my child's behaviors and hospitalizations and to plead my case as to why Lilo was the perfect candidate for their program. After days of devoting every minute to finishing the application and ensuring every "i" was dotted and "t" crossed, I officially submitted the application on August 29, 2017. It was the Tuesday before Labor Day weekend.

I will never forget the day I found out Lilo was accepted. It was late afternoon on Thursday, August 31, and I was picking up Brooke from school to take her to dance practice. While I was in the parking lot waiting for the final school bell to ring, the admissions director called to tell me Lilo had been accepted. She told me very matter-of-factly that they would be ready for Lilo's arrival on Tuesday, September 5. Without a moment of hesitation, I requested they accept Lilo immediately. I was very definitely concerned about keeping Lilo safe over the holiday weekend. However, I was especially concerned that if the weekend went even remotely well, I would decide not to send them. I was afraid I would delude myself into thinking I could handle it. Nothing could have been further from the truth, so I doubled down and stuck to my guns. Lilo needed daily professional help, and Sarah, Brooke, and I needed time to heal from the trauma. Therefore, I made the gut-wrenching decision to send Lilo that very evening.

I snuck down into the basement to hide from Lilo. I wanted to eliminate the possibility of being overheard while I made several calls to set up the transportation. Lilo had threatened to jump from my moving car if I ever tried to transport them to a residential treatment center. Thus, it was not an option for me to make the eight-hour drive to Missouri to deliver them myself. Within a couple of hours, I had a professional transportation service scheduled to arrive at the house at 2:00 a.m. the very next day. I had been counseled not to inform Lilo of the placement or the car coming to get them. The next few hours proved to be a few of the most agonizing of my life.

I was encouraged to tell no one of the plans to have my child transported out of state until they were on their way. I was, however, instructed to talk to Brooke just before she went to bed that evening. I had forewarned her that if things went badly and the transportation team had to forcibly load Lilo into their vehicle, we had to jump into my car and drive away.

Lilo is a very sound sleeper. I had no problem tiptoeing into their room with a flashlight to pack their bags. They didn't bat an eyelash. I had a hand-scrawled list of oddly specific numbers of clothing items they were allowed to take with them: six pairs of pants, eight pairs of socks, and two pairs of shoes. Every clothing item had to be meticulously labeled. I packed their bags and then silently crept downstairs to wait for the inevitable.

I was absolutely sick to my stomach as I watched the beam of headlights pull up in front of the house. They parked on the street, where the sidewalk leads directly to our front door. It was surreal and heartbreaking to know that in a matter of minutes, Lilo would be gone, and by the next morning, they would be hundreds of miles away from me. When the team got out of the car, they were all business. The three transporters walked straight up the sidewalk and into the door. They grabbed the two bags I had packed and loaded them into the vehicle so that everything was ready for a quick and immediate departure.

Then I had to face the moment I had been dreading for hours. I led a team of two intimidating bouncer types—one male and one female—plus one much smaller male, who looked more like a preppy first-year college student than a hired transporter, upstairs into my child's bedroom in the middle of the night. Lilo slept in a loft bed, so when they opened their eyes, they would be eye to eye with these three complete strangers. Immediately, I jumped onto the ladder to ensure I would be the one waking them and also be the first person they would see. Lilo was more than a bit startled by these hulking figures standing in the middle of their room. They woke up and said, "I wanted to choose a residential school together." When Lilo realized there was no other way to keep them safe, they relented a little, looked up at me, and asked an innocent question. "Do they have dogs at this school?" I reassured them that they did and explained that the canine program was one significant reason I had chosen this facility. Ultimately, I think this gave them the strength to get out of bed.

I have always been grateful for Lilo's behavior and demeanor that night. To their credit, they could have made it horrendous. It was bad enough having strangers in my house to cart my child off into the night, but I was beyond relieved that these strangers would not be dragging them against their will. Lilo was not angry. Brooke woke up, and Lilo hugged us both and continued to tell us how much they loved us. I tried my best to remain calm, but to say I was distraught and heartbroken underneath the veneer of a parent in complete control would be a gross understatement.

As soon as they left, I wanted to rush the door and tell them to bring Lilo back—feign some excuse and tell them that I'd changed my mind. I wanted to stop them with everything in my body. But then I started running through the instructions the doctors and intake nurses at the hospitals had given me. I remembered the desperation I felt as I put away anything that could be dangerous. Conversations with Priscilla began to circle around my mind. I recalled the years of terror and the deep pit in my stomach that was present every morning I awoke. Although Lilo was not even old enough to drive, I hid my wallet and my car keys so they couldn't steal money and attempt to drive away. These thoughts flooded my mind, as I reaffirmed my resolve to keep Lilo safe by sending them away. If Lilo hadn't gone with them that night, there is no question in my mind that they would not be alive today.

Brooke and I sat on the stairs as Lilo and the transport team walked out the front door. Lilo had a blanket and a pillow in the backseat with them. I left the door open because there was absolutely no way I was going to close the door on my child. They sat in the car at the foot of my sidewalk for about ten minutes. Each minute felt like an eternity. I was desperate and just needed them to pull away because I was struggling to combat every motherly instinct that was screaming at me to run out the door and rescue Lilo.

Tears streamed down my face. I was utterly hysterical. Exasperated, I choked out the words, "Your dad and I didn't adopt them so that I would give them away again!" As the car drove off into the shadowy distance, Brooke looked at me and said something I will never forget. "Mom, we're not giving them up. *We're letting them go so we can love them forever.*"

Chapter 12

LILO

I will climb a tree and call it mine, but it will fall within time.
—Lilo Baurer

I was home from inpatient for just twenty hours before I was awoken in the middle of the night by my mother abruptly turning on the lights in my bedroom. She looked worried. I asked her what was going on as my eyes were adjusting to the harsh light. She said I needed to get up. She walked away with tears in her eyes as three strangers marched into my room.

I remember being annoyed that they had their dirty black boots on my clean carpet. There was a short man, a tall man, and a tall woman. They told me I was all packed and that I was going to Missouri. I realized I was getting "gooned," still half asleep. I immediately broke down in confused tears. I had a sense of hope about getting better and was excited to be home with my mom and sister Brooke.

My mind spun as I tried to process that I was being forced to leave again. I packed a few things, like my ukulele and sketchbook, and walked downstairs with the strangers. My mother cried at the front door as the transport team escorted me to the car—one person on each side of me and one behind in case I tried to take off on foot. All I could do was go willingly. I saw no point in fighting anymore.

During our seemingly never-ending drive, I was restless and sleep-deprived in the backseat. I kept track of street signs and landmarks to find my way back if I were to run away. As we pulled off the main road, I saw a sign that read Lux Residential Treatment Center. The grounds were surrounded by tall trees that looked like they had been there many years. There were students outside walking golden retrievers.

After being led inside by the transport team, I found myself in an overwhelmingly giant room. I saw a separate room with big windows and long dining tables. The open floor concept felt inviting. I was stimulated by all the vibrant colors in the room that competed for my attention.

Entering that new treatment facility alone without any notice or opportunity to do any research beforehand was terrifying. The staff took my bags to be checked, and a nurse took me into a room with her and another female staff member. I was told to undress before them as they watched, squatting and coughing to assure them I wasn't hiding anything inside my body. They examined me for scars to record in their files and then let me get dressed. I felt completely violated.

After this humiliating experience, I met the girls in my team home, the "Explorers." They were up in a loft with a pool table and beanbag chairs. Some of them immediately started asking me questions about why I was there. Others sat in the corner observing or doing their own thing. There were seven of them, not including me. I noticed one girl was wearing a green shirt.

The shirt signaled that she was a possible threat to herself or others. It also meant she had to be within six feet of a staff member at all times, count out loud in the bathroom, and shower with the door cracked, so the staff could watch her peripherally. If someone had a green shirt, they had to sleep in the middle of the team home on a mattress on the floor instead of in a bunk, and they lost the privilege to go on off-campus outings.

A yellow shirt symbolized therapeutic safety precautions, which weren't as strict. Students were put on therapeutic for things like passing notes to the boys in the main room upstairs. To remove these precautions, you had to be approved by your therapist. Every treatment center has some system for keeping students safe. Still, when you are wearing these shirts, it feels like your insecurities are on display to the entire school. These methods invited shame.

As the first week went on, I was forced to adapt to a rigid and controlled environment. All the Explorers wrote letters to their parents and were allowed weekly phone calls—except for me, as I, a new student, was not permitted to speak to my mother, whom I resented anyway for sending me away. I was so angry with her for making me feel so alone, but I couldn't express it to her. I also couldn't go to the bathroom without someone knowing where I was. I wasn't allowed to sleep outside the view of the cameras, which monitored me 24/7 and violated every bit of privacy I once had. I was trapped physically and mentally. It was a loneliness that, over time, became unbearable for me.

After a few weeks, I found the courage to write my mother a few letters. They were filled with absolute hate. I couldn't understand why she was doing this to me again. It felt like she'd rather let the professionals try to fix me than actually try to love me. I was hurt and wanted her to hold me through it all. Being sent away brought up my attachment issues and my fear of abandonment. Eventually, I was allowed a monitored phone call with my mother. My blood boiled at her calm tone on the other line. I could hear in her voice how she pitied me. I screamed at her for giving up on me. The staff stepped in and ended the call early before I went into a full-blown panic attack.

The Explorers often walked outside the grounds when our team home had free time. It was a breath of fresh air from what felt like a cage. Walking off campus, even if it was just along the perimeter, gave us a sense of freedom. Stuck on a peninsula surrounded by water, my mind slowly felt claustrophobic in this forced therapeutic environment. On my walks, I noticed how some of the rocks would glisten on the side of the road. Eventually, I realized the glistening was caused by small pieces of broken glass.

When the staff member walking with us was busy talking to the other students, I'd slowly fall behind the group and sneak these fragments into my pockets. They were the only things that made me want to keep living. They satisfied my suicidal ideation faster than any therapist could. Ironically, finding instruments of self-harm became my way of surviving. I slowly felt more hopeless each day, so I cut myself with a tiny piece of glass about a month into the program. I was given a green shirt for the first time.

Hours after my injury, I noticed a new student had arrived. Despite the faraway glance, I knew I would like them—inside and out. I overheard the staff calling them KP and saying they were in a *violent assist.* An assist was the general term for all the physical restraints the staff were trained to perform for our or others' safety. KP's assist lasted forty-eight hours, which was unheard of. Most lasted thirty minutes at most.

The next evening, I confessed to a staff member that I was having suicidal thoughts. I didn't feel safe with myself anymore. I *thought* I would be seen by a counselor. But I was *very* wrong. Instead, I was taken to a lockdown version of a team home for anyone more of an immediate threat to themselves or someone else. There were many more staff members in this area. I later learned it was used as a punishment rather than to ensure our safety. I entered this dark team home at night, disoriented by a headache from crying while speaking of my suicidality and my eyes trying to adjust to the darkness. They walked me over to a mattress on the floor, holding onto my arms so I wouldn't trip. Exhausted from the past two days of no privacy and trying to keep it together, I soon fell asleep to the sound of a Sam Smith playlist echoing from across the room.

The next morning, I woke up in the lockdown team home they called the "Seals." There were no cabinets for our things. Everyone had their bedding and maybe a journal. The three showers had wooden, unlockable doors, none with lights because someone had broken one for the shards in the past. We showered in the dark while counting so the staff could hear a difference in our voice if we winced from pain while self-harming and to make sure we weren't trying to kill ourselves in the only privacy we had. All day, we just hung out on couches, ate, slept, and went to the bathroom—all in the same building. No one left unless approved by their therapist. Our only entertainment was fighting with each other or staff or watching the rest of the students in the other team homes through the windows.

My stay at this team home lasted three months. While there, I connected with some of the other students. I especially grew close to KP. KP was attractive, shared many stories, and was extremely suicidal. They taught me how to cut myself with paper, which was one of the few things we had access to, and they showed me how to strangle myself with the air-conditioner cords.

I quickly learned that by acting out, staff started to care a little more about your well-being. The worse we were, the more attention we got. It was sad that we all had to hurt ourselves (or one another) to talk to someone, but that was the reality of the situation. If you weren't an urgent matter, then you didn't matter at all.

I found strangling myself gave me an adrenaline rush. I let KP physically hurt me one time so that they wouldn't hurt themself. They didn't stop hurting me after that; they bit my arms a lot, and I still have the scars. Bored, I had a competition with the other teens to see who could go the longest without showering as a form of entertainment. I'd fallen into despair in my mind, and there was no ladder to climb out.

I spent Christmas in the Seals team home. I was allowed to call my mother, but I could only scream at her. I blamed her for everything I was going through and told her I hated her. Thankfully, my mother has always been one to see through my theatrics by not allowing my horrible words to push her away.

Bullying and physical violence were frequent among the students. I often witnessed students instigate physical fights with other students. I watched as a seventeen-year-old student attacked a preteen. A staff member failed to intervene; therefore, I threw myself on top of the preteen to protect her.

While lying on my bunk one afternoon, a girl I barely knew came over to my bed, hidden from view behind a wall. She got on top of me and started sexually assaulting me. I repeatedly told her "no" and forcefully told her to get off of me. Despite my lack of consent, she continued to pin my arms down so I couldn't move. As the assault was happening, my body became heavy. Physically and emotionally, I felt trapped. I was completely paralyzed, and internally, I was defeated. They say that your body goes into fight, flight, or freeze in times of stress. I was frozen and wanted to hide more than any other time in my life. While the experience only lasted a few minutes, the effects lingered. I felt incredibly unsafe after that and knew I wasn't the only one.

I grew closer to KP. They told me some of their deepest life secrets, which created a false sense of trust between us and what I was later told was an abusive relationship. I genuinely cared for and loved them; they took advantage of that. KP was so broken inside; I wanted to help them see some light in life. We had considered ourselves to be dating for about two months, but they never cared for me the way I did for them. I was in constant pain when I knew KP, but they had something that drew me to them.

After a call with their parents, KP told me they were being pulled from the program and would be leaving the next day. KP was becoming increasingly violent and had even broken a staff member's nose in an assist earlier in the week. I remember the sadness, anger, and hurt I felt when I was told they'd be leaving me. I felt like my ribs were caving in, and I would lose the ability to breathe any second. We cried together a lot, and they wrote to me in my journal before the night ended. We had a real connection. And even though they couldn't express their emotions outwardly, I still felt more loved by them than my mother during this difficult time in my life.

After KP left, I gave in to the program. I was transferred back to the Explorers, and I did my schoolwork. My mom and I were allowed off-campus visits during which she could stay with me in a hotel for a weekend. She also visited for parents' weekends. I slowly stopped saying I hated her because her visits were what I looked forward to the most. One of the most memorable weekends was when I read a poem, "Twinkling Bits of Hope," that I had written about my father. Hearing my poem, my mother reconnected with me for the first time in a long time. Before she left after that weekend visit, we had a family session on campus with Shelly, my therapist. This was the first time my mother told me a tiny bit of information about my birth family. She showed me a close-up picture of my birth mother and told me her name. This was the most I'd ever learned about my birth family. The session was extremely emotional for us, and I was angry that she knew things about me but always told me that she didn't.

I learned from Shelly that adoption was my first trauma, although it never seemed to impact me as much as my father's death. She explained that in the womb, you learn to know your mother's scent, her voice, the way she laughs and cries—she is familiar. Adopted from birth, I was placed into someone else's arms. Being stripped of that familiarity from my first breath was a traumatic experience. This is where my attachment issues and feelings of abandonment originated. She helped me realize the validity of feeling unloved all the time. It was a response to trauma that started the first time I opened my eyes, and it was no one's fault.

A hopeless feeling that stemmed from a fear of being forgotten by everyone back home kept resurfacing. I was drowning. I had heard the girls in my team home mention how a previous student had attempted to jump off the back deck down a brick-covered slope leading to the lake. I had been fixating on the image of myself jumping off that same deck. I imagined different ways I could attempt it every day. Thinking about the emotional pain ending was a coping mechanism—and once my mind was fixated on that, I couldn't stop it.

The evening sky was rolling in above my team home, and everyone was occupied with their nightly hygiene routines. I felt so lost and abandoned by anyone who tried to prove their love for me by forcing me to live. I decided to follow through with my plan. I walked out the glass door that connected my team home to the back deck. I walked to the edge, my adrenaline pumping, and hoisted myself onto the railing with my back facing the drop I intended to take. With my legs now dangling, my body physically started to shake.

I watched the glass door swing open as one of the Explorers approached. Her eyes widened as she saw me gripping tight onto the wooden rail I was seated upon. I threatened that I would jump unless she stopped coming closer. She slowly approached and sat down cross-legged a few feet away from me. She tried to talk me out of jumping as a staff member walked out and assessed what was happening. I told him to not come one step closer. He was trying to calm me down. His voice kept fading in and out. I saw another staff member heading toward me from beneath me. As he got closer, my adrenaline surged. He made me feel like I was running out of time because he would catch me and ruin my attempt. I could no longer hear what anyone was saying to me. I leaned back, and gravity took me over the edge.

I fell onto a pile of rocks and bricks that lined the hill. There was a sharp pain in my back as I tumbled down the hill. All I could think was, "I'm so stupid. Why did I think that would work?" I wanted to land on my head but when I fell, I hesitated, which changed my body's position. When I stopped rolling, I found myself pinned to the ground by heavy bricks. A staff member ran to me and began pulling them off. We sat there as I cried and expressed my anger for thinking the fall would kill me. He walked me to the nurse's station. Besides a few scratches, I wasn't hurt. The nurse said I was lucky and could've been severely wounded had I landed any other way. They took me to lockdown again, where I stayed for another three months.

After a certain point, I learned to love the physical touch and emotional release from being assisted. I often got myself into assists on purpose. I would fight staff until they pinned me down so well that I'd give up and sob. Maintaining such pressure is a tactic to help reset the nervous system, slow blood flow, and calm the person. It often helps feelings and emotions to pass.

Along with assists, I also found my desire to attempt suicide higher than ever before. During much of my residency, I consistently attempted to kill myself. I had been cutting myself with glass fragments and trying to strangle myself with air-conditioner cords. I drank a bottle of cleaning fluid thinking it might just kill me—it was very toxic and caused me to throw up for hours, while a staff member watched and laughed at me. I vividly remember her say, "You did this to yourself," while smiling as if me wanting to die was a joke. This was my new normal.

After almost a year, I engaged in Lux's canine program. The premise is that caring for a pet can be great self-care. After much hard work proving that I was responsible, I was the first to be allowed to care for a golden retriever puppy full time, as a new litter of puppies had just become available.

I walked into the kennel at the end of the hall and joined a group of nine puppies. One followed me everywhere I went, jumping on me and trying to launch himself into my arms. I knew he was meant to be mine; he chose me. I named him Tyson, and he renewed my sense of purpose and hope. This bundle of joy and golden fur made me feel more like myself again.

When all the team homes went on an adventure therapy trip for a day, I had to put Tyson in one of the kennels because I didn't have anyone to watch him. We spent the day tubing and water skiing. It was the first time I'd been tubing since my dad died. It felt amazing, and I could feel his presence on the lake. After a great day, we all exited the vans and walked down the hill back to campus. One of my friends came running toward me, screaming, "Tyson got bit!" I panicked and sprinted to the kennels. Tyson had a hole through his ear and a deep wound to his leg that required stitches. He was bloody and pretty shaken but survived the attack. I spent a full week trying to convince the canine staff that he needed stitches before they brought him to our nurse, who distributed our medications. She confirmed he definitely needed stitches. This shared trauma bonded Tyson and me. After his recovery, I helped him feel safe, and he helped me feel safe too. Tyson is the very best thing to come from this program.

One of the worst things at Lux was the Launch program, a weekend stay with your family in a house near campus. A special team from off campus joined your family and therapists to deep dive into your trauma and, through intense emotional work, reduce your stay at Lux. To make matters worse, my therapist, Shelly, was leaving Lux due to personal reasons. Karen was hired as a new therapist and assigned to me. I disliked Karen, and so did my mother. Karen and Shelly, who was trying to ease our transition into Karen's care, were both part of my Launch team. There was a specialized Launch therapist and another therapist in training present as well. The weekend was so traumatic that I blocked what happened from my memory for years. All I can remember was screaming and crying to return to Lux the first day.

Within a few months, I was allowed home visits so my transition from residential back home wouldn't be overwhelming. It started with weekend visits and then progressed to a couple of weeks at a time. However, I was still struggling to understand who I was. I had spent so much time in isolation and lockdown that I missed a lot of therapeutic work. I found it hard to ignore certain feelings about my gender identity. I expressed that I wanted to be called "Lilo," my nickname from my dad. Shortly after that, I came out as gender fluid and shaved my head.

At Thanksgiving, I was told my transition ceremony from the Lux program was scheduled for December 17, 2018. My therapist, mother, teachers, staff, and some friends would all speak about my growth while in the program. Additionally, I would officially adopt Tyson and take him home. I told my mom and Karen I wasn't ready, but they believed the transition ceremony would give me closure and help me move forward.

The ceremony went well. I was very emotional about leaving people with whom I had grown so close. I was also scared to start a new chapter of my life. My gut told me I wasn't truly healed; I was progressing but felt I was being pulled from the program too soon. No one understood why I felt this way, so I trusted the professionals and my mom. I left the facility after a sixteen-month stay, with my dog, Sarah, and my mom next to me. I was terrified but hopeful without realizing how the trauma I had been through at Lux truly affected me.

Chapter 13

MARGARET

Missouri's state motto is *salus populi suprema lex esto,* which translates to "the safety of the people should be the supreme law." Safety is exactly what I was praying for as I watched the car pull away from my house in the predawn on the first day of September. Remember, Missouri is the state Jeff and I could not wait to cross into on our way home from Arkansas after adopting Lilo. However, after Lilo's sixteen-month residential placement there, I would later want nothing more than to get out and stay out.

In all fairness, the first six to eight months were very promising, and I remained quite hopeful. Lilo enjoyed canine therapy and was working hard to earn the privilege of possibly adopting their own golden retriever while in residency. One of the most exciting days on campus was when a new litter of puppies arrived. Lilo was also actively participating in adventure therapy and had many opportunities to hike, swim, and canoe. Their residential campus was nestled back in the trees. The main building of the campus housed several team homes for both boys and girls as well as shared community space and the cafeteria. The students were then assigned to a particular home based on age and personality fit with the other team home members and team leader. Lilo's team home had a deck that faced the lake, where the school had its own private dock.

Academically, Lilo seemed to be thriving as well. The school was across the parking lot from the main building. The teachers seemed to truly enjoy their students. Lilo especially liked English because the class gave them the most opportunity to journal and write poetry.

During these first months, the honeymoon phase came to an end, and Lilo became acutely aware that there was a lot of hard work to be done between individual, group, and family therapy. We both had many assignments to complete to move through the program levels. As Lilo moved successfully through the program, they earned the staff's trust and more privileges—the ability to move more freely throughout the campus, additional privacy in the team home, and time with the dogs. I felt they had been placed in the appropriate team home with a wonderful team lead. We both had developed a great rapport with our family therapist, Shelly, and Lilo was also beginning to build trust with the day and evening staff members.

Things began to unravel by the spring of 2018. I had made the eight-hour drive several times to and from campus for visits and parents' weekends. For teens who are dealing with attachment disorders and mental health problems, change is a major influencer in bad behavior. Any change—even one that may appear small on the surface—has the potential to cause these teens to act out negatively. I learned from professionals that change can trigger deeply rooted attachment issues surrounding feelings of abandonment. For a facility that caters to adopted teens, a steady stream of fresh faces wearing staff uniforms certainly doesn't help any of their issues.

My child was very much affected by the changes. Their neurotherapist was the first to move to another location. Lilo's team lead then moved into a vacancy on campus. But our greatest disappointment came when Shelly decided to leave for personal reasons. Probably more than most, I understood that life happens, but my concern was the new therapist that was hired to replace Shelly. I knew she would not work from the moment Lilo and I met her. Our personalities seemed to clash, and neither Lilo nor I felt any natural connection, which was absolutely necessary to progress. I pleaded to be reassigned to one of the other family therapists, but I received the answer that was becoming all too familiar in this industry: "I am sorry, but the other therapists have a full caseload."

During this time, I was also highly encouraged to participate in an optional three-day program intended to expedite the healing process for each individual family. This program, Launch, not only was expensive but was also in addition to the monthly residential fee. Launch was designed to provide uninterrupted, intensive therapy by our assigned therapist and a specially trained program therapist, who together facilitated the treatment for our family.

The family (which was just me) moved into a designated house used solely for this program. The house was large, with the primary bedroom on one side and two additional bedrooms on the other. What I remember most was the expansive deck that extended the full length of the house with a small screened-in porch on one end that overlooked the wooded lot.

I went in feeling very optimistic about the experience. On the first day, I had a one-on-one with each therapist participating in Launch. The intention was to understand our family dynamic and hear our family's experience with Lilo's mental health from my perspective. I quickly learned that the timing of this program was less than ideal. The school was in transition, so Lilo's new therapist, Karen, came to shadow Shelly, who would soon be leaving the school. *Again, the timing was less than perfect.* I was outnumbered four to one, which was more than intimidating. In addition to Shelly and Karen, the program specialist would be facilitating and another therapist observing. Although I was in the presence of four mental health professionals, Shelly was the only person in the room who had any experience actually working with Lilo or me.

If I said I was willing to try *anything* to ensure Lilo was safe, it would be the understatement of the century. The "homework" for parents who rely on the troubled-teen industry to keep their children safe seemed to be never-ending. I was given two assignments that were fairly simple on the surface. The first was to write about Lilo's best day of their life. But the second assignment left me dumbfounded. I was instructed to chronicle the worst day of their life in painstaking detail, with one important caveat: *it had to be about the day they were adopted*—absolutely no exceptions. The theory behind this assignment was that their placement into my arms marked the traumatic moment when they were abandoned by their birth mother, the root cause of their attachment and relationship issues. How could I possibly write that one of the happiest days of my life was Lilo's worst day? I pleaded with the staff to let me write about the day we lost Jeff—the hardest day my family had ever lived. The instructions for the assignment were clear, and my hands were tied. I was uncomfortable and didn't want any part of this, but I reluctantly completed the assignment as instructed.

The army of therapists had already arrived when Lilo entered the house the next morning. I was asked to read the two stories to Lilo. My child responded exactly as I had predicted and warned that they would. They were beyond livid and distraught. Lilo couldn't understand why I hadn't written about their father's death. They also assumed that because their adoption was supposedly their worst day, it must have been mine.

In a turn of poetic justice, the day I was asked to read the story about Lilo's worst day became one of my worst days. Lilo was completely unresponsive to any attempts made by the therapists in the room to intervene. They felt betrayed by me. Shelly jumped in, but the presence of the other therapists only escalated things. Lilo left the house in a fit of rage and was categorically inconsolable. This exorbitantly expensive program was a failure of epic proportions.

I left the program thirty-six hours early. The therapists wanted me to stay and "work on myself," but I was as devastated as my child. In addition to this assignment, a few other family activities failed just as miserably. The Launch specialist's perception of my child's future was both startling and terrifying. She stated that Lilo would not successfully become independent, probably would not hold a steady job, and would sabotage any relationships as soon as they became too serious or stable. College probably was not in their future either. It took both Lilo and me a long time to come back from this experience. I returned home unable to eat or sleep. I began to drop weight and found it very difficult to reengage with life back home. Priscilla willingly met with me more frequently to help me process. In fact, Priscilla very recently shared that she was never more concerned about me or my well-being than she was upon my return from this program.

Although I was not immediately aware at the time, this experience marked the beginning of the end of our time in Missouri.

Following the Launch experience, my relationship with Lilo completely deteriorated beyond recognition. During the remaining few months in the *Show-Me State,* I felt like I was being shown a highlight reel of bad news and poor behavior. Every time I saw the school's area code flash across my cell-phone screen, my heart sank. I would usually waffle back and forth, weighing my options about whether I should answer. Picking up meant I was going to be told something I most likely didn't want to hear. But letting it go to voicemail meant waiting for an unknown staff member to leave a lengthy message about my child.

If the school made an unscheduled call, trouble was brewing. Each call was so appalling that I didn't recognize the person they described. I sat in stunned silence as I was told that my child had jumped off a two-story deck, drank an entire bottle of cleaning fluid, and attempted to throw themself through a plate glass window. How was this happening? I was confused, fuming, and deeply hurt that I had made what felt like the wrong decision in providing Lilo the care they needed. Lilo wasn't the only student who was deeply affected by the changes at the school, but I naively thought that in this very controlled environment, none of these antics could happen.

I continued to travel back and forth to visit Lilo or bring them home for periodic visits. What became nearly impossible to explain, and for family and friends to understand, was that I existed in two very different worlds. At home, I volunteered and attended school events and dance competitions for Brooke. I spent the occasional weekend with Sarah at her university for parents' weekend. On the road to Missouri, however, I entered a different world. The bridge in Jefferson City became my gateway into the chaotic world with Lilo. I spent most of the hours in the car in tears, fearful of what I might experience once I arrived. The unknown was frightening, but I would have to be "on" to support them and participate in our therapeutic activities.

I would be emotionally exhausted on the drive home but had to shut this part of myself "off" to function as the parent Sarah and

Brooke needed. My decisions impacted them in ways I couldn't anticipate. Sarah was in college during the darkest times, but I did not fully understand Brooke's fear until much later. They did everything they could to add no additional stress or chaos to my life. I did not realize the shriveled flower Brooke had become until she began to blossom and flourish once Lilo was out of our home.

Heading to Illinois, I couldn't wait to cross the bridge at Jefferson City, which now served as my gateway to home. Priscilla would often be on the phone with me while I transitioned from one world to the other. At this point, I was working with her on my own therapeutic development. I was trying to cope with my grief and my child's mental health struggles. I became an automaton, stuck in autopilot.

My travel to support Lilo was taking an enormous toll on my other two as well, most especially Brooke. Each trip to Missouri meant I had to farm Brooke out to family members or friends. This caused a disruption in what was finally becoming a "normal" routine following Lilo's departure. Our house was now free from the chaos. However, in addition to frequent trips to Lux, I was required to complete therapeutic homework assignments and virtually participate in family therapy. Lilo was hundreds of miles away from home yet still demanded much of my attention. Brooke was thriving in the absence of mayhem, but she was also becoming increasingly resentful of Lilo's needs.

What's more, I didn't have the relationship I wanted with Lilo, and it was hard to feel like I was doing the right thing. The desperation parents find themselves in when we can't keep our children safe in our own homes is beyond devastating. I had witnessed such highly dysregulated behavior, and I often thought that if these kids could channel their creative energy into something positive, we would have a cure for cancer. They were so industrious, and through their traumatic life experiences, they had learned how to turn a pillow into a blade. I am still absolutely primed and programmed to respond to certain situations in a fight-or-flight response. It's an old, anxious habit that served as protection during the hardest parts of Lilo's treatment. But it has been difficult to let go of this defense mechanism in the aftermath.

However, during this time of darkness came one very bright light: Tyson. He was one of a large litter of golden retriever puppies that arrived in the early summer of 2018. Lilo was seriously considering training and then adopting one of these pups. They were finding it difficult to choose one, but he had no problem instantly choosing Lilo. There was absolutely no denying their connection to one another, and he began accompanying Lilo home on visits.

Tyson's first home visit with Lilo—Fall 2018

As time wore on, it was becoming increasingly more difficult to return Lilo and Tyson back to school following a home visit. As predicted, Lilo and I were both unable to establish any type of trusting relationship with their new therapist. Changes continued to occur at the school, and ultimately Lilo was moved into a new team home. We would take a few steps forward while they were home, but their behavior deteriorated, and we would fall many steps backward upon returning to Missouri. It was becoming abundantly clear that this school was no longer a fit. Whether Lilo was ready or not, and with Tyson in tow, it was time to bring my child home.

Chapter 14

LILO

I watched helplessly as the porcelain tub began to turn red in my peripheral vision. Slowly at first, then all at once. My eyes closed as I inhaled deeply, and my mind was so empty it began to scare me. Blood dripped from the blade of a pencil sharpener that I used to mutilate my arm. All I could do was wonder why I still couldn't feel anything. I wanted to feel something again. I hadn't even felt the blade's deep incisions as I cut my left forearm.

One arm complete, I put the blade down on the side of the bathtub to pause before starting on the opposite arm. I would need to use my left hand, which was nondominant and already losing blood, so I took a moment to brace myself. Unable to think any thoughts at all, I stared blankly ahead at the faucet that was now being turned on by a hand that wasn't my own.

My mother was in the bathroom now, and I watched as her lips moved, but I couldn't understand what she was saying to me. She quickly wrapped my arm in a towel and put my opposite hand over it to show me that my open cuts needed pressure to stop bleeding. She began scrubbing the blood off the tub and down the drain. My auditory abilities and an adrenaline rush began to kick in. She said the bathroom looked like a murder scene, and she frantically tried to clean it before Sarah and Brooke got home from grabbing ice cream. She took me to the emergency room as soon as I was cleaned up.

The car ride was a blur of lights and sounds, but nothing was able to penetrate the extreme numbness I was feeling inside. I am told the hospital only stitched one of the cuts where I had nicked an artery because I was threatening to rip out the stitches. But I have no recollection of that. After they stopped the bleeding and tended to each cut, I was transferred by ambulance to an inpatient hospital.

I had only lasted one day at home after being released from Lux. I attempted suicide to avoid the anxiety and unfamiliarity of being home again after such a long stay in residential. After years of treatment, lockdown facilities had started to feel more like home to me than my childhood home, even with all the chaos and trauma. Being surrounded by people who fought for my life every day made me feel safe. Chaos was normal. Instability at home and the stress of going to school again and being with kids my age who didn't have mental health disorders or learning disabilities were terrifying. I cut to go back to the places where I felt I belonged. When I went to the hospital, I introduced myself as Lilo for the first time, and that's when people started addressing me correctly.

I was admitted to Brookview on December 19, 2018. One of my first vivid memories at the facility is spending Christmas there alone. My mother went to our family's annual Christmas celebration without me. A couple other kids in my unit didn't have a family to spend the holiday with, so we played board games at a table in the corner of the dining area. We observed patients, parents, and loved ones feasting on the hospital's Christmas dinner. I felt alone and abandoned by my mom in a world where no place felt quite right.

At some point during my stay there, I found a nail in the cafeteria peeking out from beneath a garbage can. I seized the opportunity by pocketing the nail in my sweatshirt to harm myself later. I learned to seize these opportunities while at Lux, so pocketing this nail was automatic for me.

In the privacy of my room that evening, I dug the nail into one of the wounds that had landed me in the hospital in the first place. It didn't bleed much as I twisted it deep enough into my arm to see only the top when I was done. Looking back, the saddest part of this is that I was proud of myself. I was on many medications from Lux, including antipsychotics prescribed at doses too high for my disorders. In my mind at the time, I was being funny. I walked up to a nurse on duty in the hallway and told her I was Frankenstein as I proudly displayed the nail stuck in my arm.

After that incident, I was placed on a one-to-one, where I had to be within a few feet of a staff member at all times. This was similar to precautions at Lux because I couldn't go to the bathroom alone and was watched while I slept. My stay there was a month, during which I was not attending classes. I needed to return to school so as not to fall behind further. My mother and I agreed to try a private therapeutic school, which I had attended on home visits during my time at Lux. I transitioned to outpatient at the end of January before slowly transitioning to my new school: Fusion Academy.

Fusion was a big transition for me. I was now living at home and attending therapeutic school at Fusion during the day. The whole approach of Fusion was different from any other academic setting I'd experienced before. I loved attending school at Fusion because the teachers helped make their students' hopes and passions a reality.

Fusion had one-on-one teaching, as it was a small school for kids with mental health issues or academic challenges and those needing a more intensive learning environment. Fusion also educated students "too gifted" for public schools and those pursuing extreme sports that needed a school while training. Not all students had "issues."

The teachers taught at my pace. I didn't have to feel embarrassed raising my hand to ask questions whenever I didn't understand a concept anymore. This also helped me create trust with my instructors. They understood how to handle emotional outbursts when I was frustrated because I didn't understand something. They encouraged me to use my strengths and helped me find confidence.

My writing and poetry teacher helped me the most. He provided information on how to get my work published, knowing I had dreamt of being an author since the third grade. As encouragement, he also gave me original copies of his books. The staff even helped me organize talent shows and start a poetry club. Here, I could express my creativity through the arts without being judged. Fusion was truly spectacular.

Fusion was a much better environment, but I was still in a very dark place internally. As I left outpatient and adjusted to the new school, Priscilla felt I needed help from someone specializing in the complexities of personality disorders and gender issues. I had been with Priscilla for seven years. She had stayed in touch every time I was home between hospitalizations, holding my mother's hand through it all. So I was angry when Priscilla told me she wanted me to try working with someone new. I couldn't understand why she wouldn't treat me anymore. I was also upset about starting over with another therapist after having at least a dozen in the past couple years. Priscilla was there for me when my dad died and while my BPD tendencies grew to dominate my everyday life. Most of all, I didn't want to lose someone else I loved who knew me on such a deep level. She always told me my presence in her life changed how she saw the world.

I was hurt and began sessions with Catherine, my new therapist specializing in LGBTQIA+ youth and BPD. I kept my walls up with Catherine for a long time and took my anger from losing Priscilla out on her in our sessions. I treated her like garbage, unable to accept that I had no say in this change. Despite my not being an active participant, Catherine uncovered that I had *gender dysphoria*. Gender dysphoria is distress and discomfort someone can experience when their biology doesn't align with their gender identity. I had already had my short haircut with shaved sides for a while, which felt more comfortable. We tried to explore the dysphoria, but I found it difficult to open up to her. I considered myself gender fluid and initially asked to be referred to with all pronouns—male, female, and gender-neutral. Catherine met me at a raw and broken point, and I felt like I was drowning again.

I had been home for about two months, and my family still walked on eggshells around me. I tried to create a routine with Fusion, sessions with Catherine, and reaching out to friends, but I didn't feel like I was meant to be on Earth anymore. Being home was overwhelming. After being gone for so long, Sarah and Brooke barely talked to me, which hurt because we were so close growing up. I didn't know my mother, sisters, old friends, Priscilla, or even myself anymore.

I was desperately craving to feel seen as spring approached. At home, I didn't have many people to interact with compared with my many interactions in treatment. I reached out to Mason, who I used to smoke pot with freshman year. He had gone through a breakup and also wanted to feel loved. I went to his house and hung out with him, but this time we kissed. I was shaking with anxiety the whole time. He kept making me uncomfortable, and I couldn't figure out why. Mason was supposed to be my "dream" guy, considering he was tall and muscular, had blond hair and blue eyes, and could sing. He stopped kissing me and said, "Why do you kiss like that?"

I was confused about what he was referring to, and then he began commenting on how I wasn't moving as we kissed. I was a child who spent high school in and out of hospitals. I had no opportunity to experiment with sexual interactions besides a quick kiss here and there while hiding from staff members. I didn't understand what he meant, which made me feel ashamed. Desperate to leave, I called my mom and had her come pick me up early. I didn't say a word the entire ride home.

The next morning, I woke up numb and hopelessly depressed. My mother went to her morning workout, which was her routine. I sat in bed and cried as she pulled out of the driveway. I felt like I had lost everything. I lost Everett and my friends. I had a new therapist and school, and my family felt like strangers. Everything was too much to handle. I wanted to feel loved and worthy, but my interaction with Mason made me feel unlovable.

With the changes, emotions, and unhealed traumas raging inside, I decided to take action. Home alone, I searched my mom's closet where I knew she hid our medications. There was a bottle of baby aspirin about two-thirds full. I downed fifty pills, counting each one as I swallowed. I didn't want to die; I wanted to return to my safe place: treatment. I acted impulsively and took a gamble, leaving my fate to the universe.

Just like all the other times before, adrenaline coursed through my veins. It was a familiar feeling that happened each time I attempted. I felt a unique surge of energy that was almost comforting. I texted Bridget that I had overdosed because I knew she was at the high school in class at that moment. She told me she couldn't leave the school. I walked down the block to my former high school and entered the front doors sobbing. I asked for my old guidance counselor from freshman year. They brought him out, and he looked shocked to see me again. I told him what I had done, and he called an ambulance.

At the ER again, my mother entered the hospital room with tears streaming down her cheeks—a familiar sight. I had never witnessed her cry before my father passed away, but now I caused her to repeatedly. I hurt everyone I loved because I couldn't handle my immense pain. To prevent the aspirin from being absorbed into my body, the ER staff had me drink charcoal, which was absolutely disgusting. Although the overdose was serious, I barely felt the effects of having too much aspirin in my system physically, but mentally and emotionally, it took its toll.

I was transported to a local inpatient hospital from the ER in an ambulance. Strapped down to a gurney, I watched the cars behind the ambulance through the window. On the ride, I again tried to memorize the roads we took in case I needed to escape later.

I was at the inpatient hospital for a month. I made it a game to see how many people at the hospital I could kiss, and I ended up covertly kissing five while under 24/7 surveillance by staff. My treatment team decided on a more long-term placement, but my mother had a different plan: waiting a few more weeks for a bed to open up at an assessment center in northern Wisconsin. In the meantime, I was sent back to Concordia Health in Indiana for a second time as a holding placement. I knew I would not be there long, but my mother needed more time and allowed the program to believe I was there for another full stay.

After just two weeks in Indiana, I was professionally transported for the third time in two months. This transport included a flight followed by an eighty-mile drive before finally reaching my next residential facility. Although this assessment program was to take thirty days, I found myself in residence there for more than three months.

My time there was almost a break from therapy. Unlike treatment, I spent my days playing sports, attending summer school, and watching movies. Outside, I could participate in water games, birdwatching, and photography. Although I had weekly therapy sessions and met with a social worker, it really wasn't a therapeutic environment. Most patients were there for court-mandated mental health testing. I was one of two teens who were sent by their families. I watched kids come and go a lot. No one else stayed for more than a month. Because of my lengthy stay, I had a kind of seniority that earned me the privilege of not only sitting in the front passenger seat of the facility's van but also choosing the music when we went on outings.

I was assessed to see whether my diagnosis was accurate and to confirm that my medications were appropriate and being prescribed at the correct dosages. It was determined that I suffer with major anxiety and depression, BPD traits, OCD tendencies, and ADHD, and struggle with attachment issues. Some medications were stopped while others were added—one reason for my longer-than-anticipated stay.

Ultimately, the recommendation from this assessment program was daily and consistent individual and group therapy at a long-term residential program. Therefore, I was to return to another long-term residential placement, similar to Lux, or I could stay where I was in their long-term residential program. My mother found a long-term option called New Haven in Saratoga Springs, Utah. By this point, I was exhausted by the thought of more treatment. But I'd also changed my mindset for the first time in my life. I would be an adult soon and needed to start to do the work. I was willing to genuinely try as I entered this new program.

On my last night before being transported to Utah by plane, a staff member who I'd grown fond of took me outside to the porch to watch the sunset. We had taken walks before in the evenings to do the same or to look at the stars. He was a very deep and wise soul, and I admired him for that.

That night, I was sad about being sent away again. But I was also hopeful because the sunset somehow made things look brighter, like before my dad died. That little reminder of beauty gave me the strength to start the next chapter of my journey.

Alive Again

Lately I've been reaching inside of my skin and molding my hidden crystals into masterpieces. I've been taking my soul and unwrapping the layers of bruised trauma from all these years and watching each part sparkle again.

Reprocessing and repurposing myself.

Letting the purpose crawl through each pore as a new epiphany arises from my lips and sings their songs to my therapist.

Euphoria has entangled its beautiful parts as I ground myself in each moment.

I'm becoming a new version, a better version, of who I never believed I'd breathe long enough to become.

I'm finally feeling alive again.

(June 2022)

Chapter 15

MARGARET

After officially adopting Tyson and following Lilo's transition ceremony in Missouri, Lilo returned home to Illinois on Monday, December 17, 2018. I was scared but also hopeful. We had recently discovered an amazing alternative school in the nearby suburb of Oak Brook: Fusion Academy. Fusion provided individual instruction as well as many creative learning opportunities within the arts. It was the perfect fit. Before their transition, Lilo had attended some classes at Fusion for a few weeks at a time during their home visits. They loved their teachers and immediately connected with the principal. Lilo especially enjoyed painting, writing poetry, and recording music in the school's recording studio. Lilo even organized and participated in a talent show there.

Knowing that Lilo was enrolled at Fusion for the start of the second semester, I was beginning to look forward to Christmas, which was just a week away. We were also excited about a family wedding on New Year's Eve. But Lilo had other plans. Barely twenty-four hours after Lilo arrived home, our family was shattered again. Lilo self-harmed so severely while in the bathtub that they nicked an artery.

Earlier that evening, Sarah and Brooke had asked Lilo to join them on a trip to get ice cream. I was surprised Lilo had turned them down, but now I knew why. I grabbed a towel and while Lilo applied pressure, I took a couple of extra moments to wipe down the bathroom. Sarah and Brooke would be home in a matter of minutes, and with blood splattered all over the walls and ceiling, our bathroom looked like a crime scene.

We jumped into my car and raced to the hospital. The moment we pulled away from the house, Lilo announced that they were feeling much better and that there was no need to head to the ER. While gritting my teeth in fear and anger, I responded, "That ship has sailed. The moment you chose to self-harm, you forced this trip to the hospital."

Upon our arrival to the ER, Lilo became very angry. With a guard planted outside their door, they were rude to the nurses trying to treat them. Lilo threatened the medical staff that if they stitched their arm, they would rip out every single stitch. The doctor decided to use glue and wrap their wound instead.

I was left numb from the scene in my bathroom and my child's disrespectful behavior. I remember walking out of their hospital room and literally sitting down on the floor around the corner. I began to sob. I had absolutely no idea what more I could possibly do to help them. A doctor found me and ushered me into a small waiting room within the emergency department after getting me a cup of coffee. I immediately texted Priscilla that we were in the hospital and asked her to call me. It wasn't long before I looked up to see Priscilla standing in the doorway.

It was getting very late, and Lilo had already fallen asleep. Priscilla and I left as the hospital continued to try to find an open bed at a nearby inpatient facility. Because Lilo was still a minor, I knew I would have to drive to their next placement in the middle of the night to sign them into the program. I was notified at 2:00 a.m. that a bed was available at a facility about thirty minutes away. Thankfully, the facility allowed me to verbally consent to Lilo's transfer, so I didn't have to appear in person.

During Lilo's sixteen-month stay in Missouri, Priscilla and I agreed to find a therapist specializing in suicidal ideation, self-harm, and high-risk behaviors. Initially, Lilo was very unhappy not to be under Priscilla's care, but eventually, they were able to form a trusting relationship with their new therapist, Catherine. Catherine warned me that Lilo's new placement, Brookview, might be a wake-up call for them. Many of the patients there were wards of the state. Brookview had a reputation for being a difficult place to endure due to the extreme behaviors and complex diagnoses of the other adolescents. She thought it might abruptly end some of Lilo's antics. It didn't.

Lilo spent the next three weeks at this facility, and I spent most days and every evening driving back and forth for visiting hours. Every time they were hospitalized, I became a prisoner to the new facility's schedule. I had to meet with therapists and the temporary psychiatrist and learn their philosophy and methods of treatment. Each new treatment center was like starting all over again. It was often nerve-racking to walk alone in the dark parking lot late at night following visiting hours. I felt safer when Tyson (now a large golden retriever) was with me. Unexpectedly, Lilo and I both connected well with one of the counselors at Brookview. Upon Lilo's discharge, this counselor offered me her assistance should I ever need it in the future. Unfortunately, I would be forced to reach out to her in just a few short weeks.

Due to this inpatient placement and then the partial hospitalization program that followed, Lilo began classes at Fusion a month later than planned. They seemed to settle in after a couple weeks. They did not always have class on Fridays, so Lilo was home on the morning of February 22, 2019. I went to my scheduled workout that I knew would only take an hour. Lilo was preparing breakfast and was then going to get ready to go with me upon my return to sign up for driver's education classes since their permit had expired. I was on my way home when my phone began to blow up. First, the mother of Lilo's good friend called me to report that Lilo had taken some sort of medication. I immediately hung up and dialed 911. The police had already dispatched emergency personnel after receiving several calls. Then, Lilo's former school counselor called me. The counselor assured me that Lilo was conscious and safe and that paramedics had already arrived at the scene. There are no words to describe my emotions as their former counselor encouraged me to drive carefully to the school.

During the hour I had been away, Lilo had gone through my closet and found a hidden bottle of low-dose aspirin. They swallowed fifty pills and then panicked. They texted their friend for help and ran over to the school. When I arrived, Lilo was being transported out of the school on a stretcher. As they were loaded into the ambulance, I was standing on the sidewalk with the school nurse on one side of me and the counselor on the other. I was frantic and had no idea if I was going to pass out or be sick.

The next thing I remember is being back in the emergency room. Lilo was then transferred to the pediatric floor of another hospital because the level of aspirin in their system was much too high. While we waited for their vitals to normalize, the search was on for an open bed in yet another inpatient program where they could be transferred upon release. Within forty-eight hours, a bed became available and Lilo was moved again to inpatient, their third suburban hospital stay in as many as three days.

At this point, it was clear that my child's behavior was becoming more impulsive and their suicidal ideation was intensifying. Our conversations became heated, and their threats became more grave. However, the inpatient staff saw an entirely different version of Lilo than the one I visited every evening. Lilo had learned how to "game" the system. They knew what to say and exactly what the medical professionals needed to hear. The hospital personnel felt they were ready to be released, so less than two weeks after ingesting fifty pills, Lilo was scheduled to be discharged on the morning of March 7.

Lilo had consistently threatened that they would attempt again and succeed once they returned home. I reported these threats on many occasions, but of course, this is not what Lilo disclosed to the psychiatrist. Therefore, there was no reason to hold them. As a minor, I was legally required to accept Lilo into my care, but I told the staff that I would refuse to take custody because of Lilo's continuing threats of suicide. I was informed that the hospital would have no other choice but to report me to the authorities if I refused custody of my desperately suicidal teen.

On the morning of the scheduled discharge, I was sitting in my car in the parking lot sobbing to Priscilla. If I were forced to leave the hospital with Lilo, I knew they would not survive. There was no way I could keep them safe in our home 24/7. I felt that I had absolutely no options. I was faced with a harrowing decision of risking my child's life or risking being arrested for negligence and child abandonment.

I was hysterical. Priscilla instructed me to get on the phone with the hospital advocate. Fighting back tears, I described in painstaking detail all that had transpired, and the advocate promised me that she would request a second opinion from a different psychiatrist.

As I waited to hear about that second opinion, I quickly devised a plan B. I called the counselor at Brookview, who had offered her help just a few weeks before. The backup plan was that I would drive Lilo back to Brookview and explain to Lilo that their PHP was starting immediately. The counselor told me to drive to a side entrance, where she would be waiting with the door open. Lilo would have to voluntarily get out of the car and willingly walk through the doors. Brookview could not legally force them, but if Lilo walked in, the counselor would admit them into their care. This would prevent Lilo from coming home where I could not keep them safe, and it would give me much-needed time to prepare a longer-term treatment arrangement.

I had been in the parking lot for so long that I was now late for Lilo's discharge meeting. I was still waiting to hear from the psychiatrist who would be providing a second opinion. But with a plan B in place, I decided to go to the meeting. I was quickly ushered into a tiny office within the unit. Lilo was in the room crying and furious with someone I had never met. It was the newly assigned psychiatrist, who had just informed Lilo that there was no way they were ready to be released. I am not the least bit ashamed to admit that I have never been more relieved in my life or more grateful to a hospital advocate. Fortunately, plan B was not necessary, and Lilo remained hospitalized based on the examination by the second psychiatrist.

These were challenging times. I can't emphasize enough how few options there are for parents who just want to keep their children safe. The insurance loopholes, the facility policies, and the mountains of paperwork are all overwhelming. I will never forget my conversation with a parent desperately seeking a safe placement for her child. Her teen was wreaking havoc in her home, and their entire family was terrified. She was struggling to find a safe placement because of bed unavailability, financial constraints, or both. In a moment of pure hopelessness, she stated that planning her child's funeral would almost be easier than finding a safe placement. Although her assertion took my breath away, I somehow understood, having experienced the very same feelings of despair and isolation.

I felt like I was in a race against the clock. I had exactly fourteen months to find the best treatment possible for my child before they became a legal adult on their eighteenth birthday. Priscilla reaffirmed that I was not alone and emphasized the importance of building a strong team to help with Lilo's care. With Lilo safely in the hospital, I hired both an educational consultant and an attorney. We all diligently went to work to decide our next steps in finding the best treatment for Lilo.

Due to the countless number of hospitalizations and placements, Lilo's medication was constantly changing. Various medications were being discontinued as new ones were introduced. If medications remained the same, their dosages were increased or decreased at what seemed to me to be an alarming rate. Keeping track of these meds and their dosages felt like my full-time job. It was our consultant who first introduced me to the idea of an assessment program. She told me about a program out of state that observed adolescents for thirty or more days to determine whether their medications and diagnoses were appropriate. I believed this was the necessary next step.

Just as I had heard so many times before, the assessment program was full, and they did not anticipate an opening until the end of April. I had researched and had many conversations with the admissions director. She became my salvation. I was certain that an assessment was needed and confident that this program was the right fit. I now had to find a placement for my child in the interim while we waited for a bed to become available.

I, too, was becoming all too familiar with the vocabulary necessary for admittance into a mental health program. I was advocating at the top of my lungs and becoming so persistent that mental health professionals in my state and around the country were tired of answering my calls. The only available bed I could find was at the Indiana facility, Concordia Health, where Lilo had spent the summer of 2017. I just needed a safe place for the next thirty to forty-five days until I could transfer Lilo to the assessment program. On March 17, 2019, Lilo left the hospital and was transported back to Indiana. I had every intention of having Lilo follow the program's curriculum while they were there, but I knew they would not be there long enough to complete it. I was using this placement as a safe house, or otherwise, the most expensive babysitting imaginable. My motive was just one: to keep Lilo alive until the assessment. As luck would have it, a bed became available much sooner than expected. I immediately arranged for professional transport to the assessment program the first week of April.

After Lilo's arrival, they were observed for a few days before the assessment team made decisions regarding the medications that seemed no longer beneficial. It was almost like a detox program. We needed a clean slate to find the right medications and dosages to achieve more consistent behavior. There can be severe psychological and physiological consequences when discontinuing the use of an antipsychotic drug. It was vitally important that Lilo be monitored and weaned from these meds carefully under strict supervision. With the knowledge that Lilo was safe for at least the next month, our educational consultant and I continued researching and gathering information about residential programs nationwide. While I began applying and interviewing with program directors, the admissions director at the assessment program was able to prove medical necessity and keep Lilo longer than the expected forty-five days. Ultimately, they assessed and treated Lilo for 102 days, long enough to safely wean them from ineffective meds and introduce much more helpful ones. Ironically, this program also had a therapeutic residential program but didn't have an open bed. I was crushed because it would have been so easy for Lilo to remain at the same location and move into the residential program with staff we both thoroughly trusted. While it seemed like a setback at the time, I believe it was a blessing in disguise.

For close to four years, I had made countless phone calls to professionals and other parents of struggling adolescents looking for the best care for my child. I had spent hundreds of hours reading and researching various programs across the country. During these discussions and my own research, one program consistently surfaced: New Haven. Our educational consultant raved about it as well. My only hesitation was its location. New Haven has two campuses in Utah. I was well aware of New Haven when I'd sent Lilo to Missouri. Missouri seemed a million miles away from our home, so the state of Utah felt like it was on another planet. Faced with very few options and with less than one year until Lilo's eighteenth birthday, I decided New Haven was worth investigating to see if the program might be a good fit.

In June 2019, I was with Sarah and Brooke in the Wisconsin Dells attending Brooke's dance competition. While there, I received a phone call from the assessment program's admissions director. She was ecstatic because a bed had just opened up in their residential unit. Coincidentally, I had spent a couple hours on the phone the day before with an admissions counselor from New Haven. I had fallen in love with her and the school and was scheduled for a virtual New Haven tour the next day. It may sound unbelievable or even a bit supernatural to some, but I truly believe Jeff played a role in this. He knew that I was struggling with the decision to send our child to Utah. Miraculously, a bed was now available where Lilo was already in residence and with a team we trusted wholeheartedly. I believe Jeff was making it possible for me to look at both programs head to head so I could make the best decision for Lilo and our family.

After returning from the Dells, I packed up Sarah, Brooke, and our dogs, Tyson and Scarlett, and headed north to visit Lilo and tour the assessment program's residential facility. The staff met with me to discuss academics, community opportunities, and program goals. I could not imagine moving Lilo away from such caring professionals who had fiercely championed for Lilo's care and a much longer than average stay. However, I believe in my heart that Jeff wanted me to see beyond the ease of leaving Lilo in their current location and with their devoted care team. I felt he wanted me to consider the whole picture: location, culture, community size, and opportunities. Excellent facilities and reputation aside, I sensed a tremendous pull to New Haven, which ultimately was the better long-term solution for our family. Feeling secure with my decision and as though I had Jeff's blessing, I began planning to transport Lilo to Saratoga Springs, Utah.

Visiting Lilo during their assessment program—
June 2019

Chapter 16

LILO

The beat-up minivan was headed away from the airport. I felt claustrophobic, squeezed in between the charcoal-colored mountains near Salt Lake City, Utah. My anxiety was heightened as the driver began telling me about where I was headed: New Haven Residential Treatment Center in Saratoga Springs. The forty-five-minute drive felt emotionally draining after my flight.

We eventually pulled in front of the campus, which consisted of two big white houses, a pasture full of horses and hay, and cats walking around (with more freedom than the students). I was taken to the nurse's station to get strip-checked for any "contraband" (self-harm objects, substances, etc.). Then, they checked in my personal belongings and brought me to a room—a "safety room"—where students are observed in order to learn their behaviors before determining the best room placement for them.

For the first few days, I stayed in the safety room, which had window blinds that could only be opened and closed from the outside. The room had its own bathroom, and staff could watch you out of their peripheral vision when you used the toilet or shower. There was a single bunk bed; I was given the bottom bunk.

As I got situated in my new room with the staff's eyes still watching me like a hawk, the bed frame creaked. My roommate, who was also on safety precautions and had arrived a few weeks before me, began waking up. I was told she'd been refusing to go to school and slept all day instead, so she remained on "safety" for not cooperating with the program.

Just then, the hallway door swung open and about ten students walked in, chatting away as they headed to the kitchen searching for snacks. With students staring at me through the big windows, I felt like a zoo animal that had invaded their territory. Some of them smiled, while others ignored me. I felt out of place with my short haircut, and my social anxiety began to skyrocket.

The staff who were with me on safety took me to get a snack and to determine which groups I'd be attending. They had groups for body-image issues, substance abuse and addiction, values, leadership, etc. After my groups were selected, I met my therapist, Melanie. She had long, wavy, blonde hair and blue eyes. I was intimidated by her at first, and I could immediately tell this place was going to be different from my other placements. I sat on her small couch in her secluded office in the basement and took in my surroundings. There were pictures of her family, some art that looked to be from other patients, framed inspirational quotes, and a bookshelf lined with therapeutic workbooks and diagnostic guides. On Melanie's desk was a small, square, laminated piece of paper that read, "You're awesome!" in rainbow-colored, cursive lettering. I quickly learned that matching random objects by color to each letter in my mind during our sessions was a good grounding technique to keep me present when our sessions became difficult.

As the weeks went on, I eventually received my own room. I began introducing myself as gender fluid and asked to be referred to by all pronouns. Only a few people respected my request by using he/him occasionally. I knew from my experiences that being called he/him felt good sometimes.

New Haven's program consisted of five distinct levels patients would progress through, safety being the first. Each level came with new privileges and meant you were closer to going home. They valued integrity there. Often, students would tell on other students to achieve their levels faster. Usually, they would tell if people were kissing in secret. As is the case with any form of mental health treatment, having a romantic relationship with another patient in any way was frowned upon because it would take your focus away from healing yourself.

New Haven's therapeutic curriculum helped us work on different parts of ourselves throughout the program. Each student was assigned a values coach who helped us complete therapeutic assignments from our treatment team, which included our individual therapist, psychiatrist, values coach, and school teacher, along with other house therapists. They all met collectively on Tuesdays and discussed each student in the house. They created new weekly assignments and decided when students were ready to receive their next-level placements. Based on our progress, they determined whether we were on track with our treatment plans and what we needed to do to stay on track.

Completing our values assignments, doing well in school, being vulnerable in therapy, and communicating honestly with our values coach were all important aspects of our treatment. Some therapy assignments and exercises I received throughout my stay were aimed to help me become more self-aware. One of them I very vividly remember dealt with a concept called "black-and-white thinking," which occurs when a person thinks in extremes. To help interrupt these negative thought patterns, my treatment team gave me several tiny samples of paint colors, ranging from white to gray. I had to write the high of my day on the white sample and the lowest moment of my day on the darkest gray sample. On all the other samples that gradually bled into gray, I wrote things throughout the day that weren't as extreme so I could practice seeing a middle ground.

New Haven was very progressive in the sense that it felt very interactive. Students could witness other students making progress, reinforcing the program's principles and philosophies. For example, one girl was dealing with overwhelming shame. Her treatment team had her pick up rocks outside to represent everything she felt shameful about: her appearance, behavior, failures, etc. Then she was instructed to label each one with a Sharpie and carry the rocks in a backpack when she walked to different locations. She told me this exercise was extremely helpful in understanding physically how heavy her shame was. The staff's recommendations taught her how much her shame weighed her down and helped her realize she needed to let go of her shame psychologically. She spent weeks working on "healing" what each rock represented metaphorically, and we all watched as she got to remove them from her backpack one at a time as she let go of the psychological burden they represented. Watching someone heal and move on from their shame was beautiful. Her courage inspired me to do the same.

I went into the program diagnosed with BPD "tendencies," as fully diagnosing me before I was eighteen would have been inappropriate. Melanie really focused on teaching me about BPD and its effect on my life. We read together, went through workbook assignments, and determined which symptoms I experienced and what behaviors I displayed. The more I learned about this disorder, the more I understood my behavior and thought processes. One of the symptoms I experienced was extreme emotional fluctuations. If someone said or did something that hurt me even slightly, my brain often said, "I should kill myself. I'm a waste of space. This pain won't end." Dealing with extreme suicidal ideation from something as minor as someone not holding the door open for me because they didn't realize I was behind them was frustrating.

I also learned more about my self-harm and self-destructive impulses while in treatment. I discovered that people with BPD can't maintain stable relationships because of this need to push and pull. I constantly wanted to feel noticed, heard, and wanted, so I would pull people in close to me by being vulnerable and open about my hardships and trauma. But when people got to know me too well or got "too close," my first reaction was invariably to push them away to protect myself from potentially being let down or abandoned if they couldn't handle the worst sides of me. Pushing away stemmed from my fear of being abandoned again because of the death I'd experienced in my childhood and the pain of separation from my birth family.

After understanding why my brain is wired the way it is, I focused on noticing the thought patterns my BPD caused in my everyday life. I quickly learned how often I fell into those patterns and what types of situations triggered them. Armed with this self-awareness, I worked with Melanie to go deeper into identifying cognitive distortions and learning how to redirect them.

I had been learning about redirecting my cognitive distortions for years in placement. The strategy had never worked because I wasn't willing to change. I also didn't understand my diagnosis enough to know what thought patterns were meant to be redirected. Learning about BPD genuinely changed my life—although it did take most of my stay to actually change my thoughts. But the more I changed, the stronger I grew, which made stepping away from my suicidal ideations easier.

A couple times at New Haven I felt so depressed that I wanted to attempt, but I didn't. The main factor that stopped me was the staff. I felt like they actually understood me. Juliet, for example, truly believed in me. When I first arrived, I had a suicidal episode, but I told Juliet before acting. She said she would put me on safety for the night until I could talk to Melanie. Still, I begged Juliet to take me to an inpatient facility, but she refused. Instead, she sat with me until I fell asleep. At the time, I couldn't understand why she would not take me to an inpatient facility. But as I learned more about BPD, I eventually came to see what she was doing.

Another major missing piece of the puzzle at this point in my life was my gender identity. Gender is such a confusing concept. Trying to find which gender feels most accurate is a process of self-discovery. Some kids know they're transgender from the moment they can speak, and I've always been jealous of them. But that's usually the case for people who are trans male or female. Gender is a spectrum that's sometimes not as clear-cut as "boy" and "girl" or "trans boy" and "trans girl." One student, Dylan, taught me a lot about myself.

Dylan is nonbinary and uses *they/them* pronouns. They knew their identity before New Haven, so everyone knew Dylan as enby. "Enby" is a term used for nonbinary people—derived from the first letters N and B—whose gender identity is not male or female. Dylan looked very androgynous, was kind, and didn't cause drama. They were good at making people smile and laugh and had a fun personality. I admired their authenticity in groups and their ability to separate themself from unnecessary drama.

After befriending Dylan, I noticed how uncomfortable I felt with my identity when people stopped using my other pronouns and also only referred to me as "girl." It was something I had felt for years, but as I practiced self-awareness, I noticed this feeling I'd been pushing away had suddenly surfaced. I started talking openly with Dylan about their journey of figuring out who they were. They were so relatable. I felt less alone talking to them. They let me ask questions, and we had several open discussions exploring what gender meant to us. I told them I didn't feel like myself, and they suggested asking the house to use gender-neutral pronouns (they/them) for a week as a trial run.

The students and staff in our house really supported Dylan, so this suggestion made sense. I asked everyone to use they/them for me for the next week. As most people obliged, I felt much more comfortable in conversations and discovered my pronouns were in fact they/them. Still, I didn't feel weird being called he/him either. I definitely wasn't a girl, but I still liked to dress femininely and felt feminine sometimes. I also dressed and felt masculine at times. Occasionally, I didn't feel either way. That's why I thought I was gender fluid at first. Maybe I identified with all genders? Dylan helped me learn that sex is very different from gender, and gender is also different from being feminine and masculine.

For example, a man who is *cisgender*—when a person's gender identity corresponds with the sex given to them at birth—might not be outwardly masculine all the time. Men can express their femininity through clothing, such as wearing skirts, or feel feminine internally but not change their physical appearance externally. Gender itself is fluid. Clothes don't have a gender; neither does being born with a specific sex. In my opinion, the idea that to be a "real" girl or boy means you have to stick to gender norms in our society is completely constructed unrealistically by cis people who truly don't understand what being trans is like.

I identify with both they/them and he/him pronouns; thus, I'm *transmasculine* (I do not identify with the gender and sex I was assigned at birth) and *nonbinary* (I do not fall within a binary gender system but rather a gender spectrum). Being nonbinary means I don't identify with any gender. I am neither a "boy" nor a "girl," but I can still express my gender identity by being masculine and feminine. For me, transmasculine means I prefer masculine terms such as "sir" and "handsome," but I am still not a boy. Understanding all this was relieving, and I finally came to terms with my identity while at New Haven.

As my transition into official adulthood approached, I often thought about moving forward as an adult without my father and living with my BPD diagnosis. I hadn't considered college or jobs because after surviving my sixteenth birthday, I promised myself I would commit suicide before my eighteenth. However, more often than not, eighteen-year-olds can sign themselves out of placement; I grew up watching older kids sign themselves in and out. I remember my younger self thinking that if given a chance, I'd definitely sign myself out. But I had chosen to cooperate and work the program to get the help I needed. This was a life-changing decision for me. I was told my months of hard work would be wasted if I signed myself out before graduation.

With only a few weeks to decide, my suicidal ideation reappeared. This time it was very intense. I had an episode where I plotted to either jump off the third-floor balcony onto concrete or hang myself. I vividly imagined hanging under the stars with the life sucked out of me. I began pacing outside underneath the balcony, attempting to calm myself, even though I wasn't supposed to be out after dark. I had a full-blown panic attack. Juliet came outside with another staff member on shift that evening. I told her what was going on in my head, and she told me she would put me on safety. I begged her to take me to an inpatient because I was scared of what I'd do to myself, but again, Juliet insisted I stay at New Haven. She let me pace until the panic attack passed, but the suicidal urges were still present. Afterward, she sat in the doorway of my bathroom while I showered. After a few hours, I went to bed in the safety room, and the suicidal ideation passed. Before the staff shift changed, I told Juliet that I didn't feel suicidal anymore. She knew I'd get through it. She wasn't ignoring my cries for help. She *believed in me*.

On my eighteenth birthday, I was brought to the front office to complete my paperwork. I legally had the choice to sign myself back in or to leave. I began to cry, knowing I needed to graduate, and signed myself back into the program. Reaching my eighteenth birthday was a milestone that meant I had chosen life. My birthday meant I'd enter adulthood fatherless. My birthday meant I actually had to consider my future.

I achieved Level 4 after signing myself in as a legal adult. This level came with certain privileges, like having daily access to my cell phone so I could call my mom. Cell phones are not allowed in most treatment centers—and when they are allowed, you must earn the privilege to use them. I also had access to Instagram again. With such newfound freedom, I had to compromise with Melanie. She was well aware of my past behavior. She knew the negative impact my old friends I might want to contact could have on me. She also knew I'd sought inappropriate attention from strangers online. We discussed wiping the slate clean and transitioning home with no friends. That idea originally felt as monumental as the world ending, but ultimately, I knew it was best. My old friends were toxic and wouldn't help me smoothly integrate back home, so I agreed.

For the rest of May, I focused on finishing school and taking finals. I identified my priorities, knowing I would be going home soon. I worked on my cognitive distortions and understanding my gender after determining I am transmasculine-nonbinary. I was anxious to leave and excited that I had so much newfound hope.

I graduated in June 2020. The ceremony included students from New Haven's south campus, which was about thirty minutes from us. We all dressed up in our caps and gowns. I painted my cap with Pride colors and the word LOVE, as it was Pride month. Parents and family could attend the ceremony (with masks on and negative COVID-19 tests). Mom, Sarah, and Brooke all flew in for me. The students who weren't graduating watched via Zoom inside their houses. I received a leadership award and an English award. I was lucky to have that ceremony when the rest of the world was shut down.

After the graduation ceremony, my family was allowed to spend another day off campus with me to prepare for my transition ceremony, which would be held later in July. We headed to *Color Me Mine,* an art store where you can decorate ceramic items. It is tradition for each family to create a tile to display on a wall outside the school. The unique tiles represent each family who has successfully

Baurer family tile for the New Haven alumni wall—
June 2020

completed the program. Some tiles contain a significant word or symbol; others have family pets. Every student aims to place their family's tile on that wall.

Sarah, Brooke, and our mom agreed we'd paint a dragonfly on our tile. Dragonflies are the symbol of transformation and new beginnings. We all wanted my coming home to be permanent this time. I would need to break the pattern of running off to treatment whenever I was scared. I would have to rebuild trust with all three of them and restart our relationships. They would have to trust that their feedback wouldn't make me feel suicidal, as I had changed my thought patterns. As we painted, I felt connected to my family again, and I didn't want them to leave. I felt ready to go back home.

I had experienced transitions from facilities before and didn't feel I needed another for closure. I begged my mom to take me on their flight home with them. I told her that I felt ready and, being eighteen,

I could legally sign out. I expressed my reservations about waiting for the transition ceremony and wasting another month in Utah. She refused to say yes, and I broke down in tears. Not wanting to cry in the store, I walked out to the parking lot. My mother followed not far behind. I found a boulder to sit on while I cried, and my mother sat silently next to me. I begged her to take me home, expressing that I was tired of her leaving me over and over again. She told me that it was just one month, and it wouldn't be worth it to leave when I was so close to the finish line.

This conversation was extremely painful for me. Recognizing that pain, my mom cried with me. Eventually, we understood each other's perspective. We were silent, taking in the mountains around us as the sun lowered. Then, a bright blue, beautiful dragonfly flew by us, and we knew my father was trying to tell us something. It flew off as we cried together again, and as soon as it was out of sight, another dragonfly flew right in front of our faces. I watched it fly toward the store, and I understood its message. The dragonflies were a sign that I needed to complete the entire program so my family could gain closure. Truly accepting myself was vital as I neared the end of my safety net.

We followed the dragonfly back to the store and hugged for several moments. We finished the dragonfly painting, with Sarah and Brooke putting the final touches on the tile. Then, they drove me back to campus, hugged me, and left me there for the last time. The decision to stay meant admitting that I had needed the treatment to be forced upon me on so many occasions. I don't regret staying.

Throughout the year in therapy, Melanie and I talked about my birth family periodically. As the end of my stay approached, I had a virtual family session with my mother. She and Melanie told me an unbelievable truth: the picture of my birth mother that my mom gave me at Lux had been cropped. The full picture was of my birth mom and three older half-siblings. For my entire life, my mom had known I had siblings and never told me. I was stunned to the point of tears.

After years of being the middle child, a blonde between two brunettes who strongly resembled each other, and feeling left out of our family because I was adopted, I had real-life, blood-related siblings. The oldest one even looked like me in the picture. I felt betrayed that my mom had lied to me for so long, but she explained that she had promised my dad they'd tell me together when I was old enough. I did my best to understand how hard that must've been for her as I felt the pain of betrayal simultaneously surging within me.

Melanie proceeded to tell me that my mom had located my birth mother. I was bawling at this point. The relief, confusion, excitement, and fear washed over me. This person I had dreamed about for years was now real. I had so many questions for her and couldn't bear to wait any longer. My mom had reached out to my birth mother to make sure she was okay with me contacting her directly. She also discussed my diagnoses and residential placement at New Haven and explained my preference for the name "Lilo." My mom requested that she not tell me everything on our first call because it could be too much to process before transitioning home.

We took the weekend to allow me time to process and prepare for the call. Late one evening, Melanie called me to her office. I had been sitting in my anxiety all day, waiting for this moment. I took a deep breath as she pressed the call button. It rang a few times before I heard a woman with a southern accent pick up and say, "Hello?" My birth mother was crying over the line.

My birth mother and I talked for about twenty minutes. She explained that two of my sisters from the picture were with her, and I got to say "hi" to them. I also had a younger half-brother who was with them too. He was ten, the age I was when my dad died. He told me he loved me, and I also told him I loved him before we ended the call. That day changed my life in so many ways. For as long as I can remember, I have felt a closed door stood in my path. Having knowledge about my birth family and background, this door has finally opened, and I have the freedom to explore. I texted and slowly began to build a relationship with each new sibling over time. I also learned that my birth father had another child.

With my transition ceremony approaching, my mother flew back to Utah on July 13, 2020. The night before she arrived, Melanie and I had our last individual session together. She gave me advice for going home with no friends—those we agreed were not good for me and others who had moved on. She told me she knew it'd be hard but she wouldn't have made me cut everyone off if she didn't believe in me. We also discussed what boundaries I would maintain with my birth family moving forward.

As we talked, I found myself staring at her small laminated "You're awesome!" sign. I made eye contact with her and started crying. She let me feel my emotions in silence before asking what was going through my head. I told her I thought the sign was tacky when I first arrived but used it to stay grounded throughout the year. I looked at her and explained that she helped me see myself again. I told her that thanks to her guidance, I finally believed the phrase "I'm awesome" for the very first time in my life. She said, "You always have been!" I thanked her for showing me that I could love myself and feel worthy again and for never giving up on me. Filled with hopes and fears for the future, we said our goodbyes.

Priscilla, Sarah, and Brooke videoconferenced in to watch my ceremony. Students and staff members, who I had personally selected, spoke about my progress and their wishes for me moving forward. My mom and I showed our family tile from the graduation trip and explained what the dragonfly means to our family. My mother spoke directly to me. She had spoken at these ceremonies before but had never looked me in the eyes and told me how she really saw me. All I have ever wanted was someone to see my pain, recognize it, and choose to stay anyway. My mother did that for years, but this was the first time I knew she truly understood. We were connected in a way we had never been before.

When Melanie finally spoke to me, she was crying. She told me how proud she was of me. Melanie always made me feel seen. When I wouldn't listen in the past, she'd get mad. No therapist had ever gotten mad at me like that before, but no therapist had helped me see myself the way Melanie did either. She was frustrated because she cared so much, and I'm so thankful for her. She left me with two gifts. One was a ring that read "I am enough," and the other was her laminated "You're awesome!" sign as a reminder that *I am awesome*.

Lilo says goodbye to Melanie—July 2020

Near the end of the ceremony, I addressed the staff and students before we watched my video slideshow, which contained family photos and pictures from my years in treatment. I used the song "See You Again" by Carrie Underwood to accompany our family pictures with my dad. The last song, "Grow as We Go," by Ben Platt, represented moving forward. To end the ceremony, the students in my house and the staff stood in a giant circle with arms around each other. I then went around the room, hugging each one of them goodbye. The last person I hugged was Melanie, and I held on for as long as I could.

My mother did not understand my feelings of not belonging before my dad passed, but afterward, we connected through similar forms of grieving. I watched her deal with her alopecia over the years and know the emotional toll it has taken. She saw my pain but didn't know how to help me. We didn't know how to communicate with one another. Still, we had an unspoken understanding that we wouldn't let each other give up, even if we didn't understand the other's perspective. Looking at my mother during the ceremony, I felt a sense of purpose. She said she would always be there for me, and for the first time, I believed her. I understood that my mom had sent me away to save me—not because she couldn't see my pain or wanted me to live out of selfishness, as I had always believed. She had faith I would find the light again.

After years of darkness, I left New Haven with hope. I left knowing I am awesome and having a real relationship with my mom for the first time in years. I would tell her when I was suicidal, and she wouldn't send me away out of fear for my life anymore. She'd sit with me until the feeling passed, just like Juliet did. She'd stop telling me what I needed to do to fix my issues. She would listen to my needs, even when she couldn't fix them. She would hear what I needed to say and let me cry on her shoulder. We would stop and smell the roses, but this time, we would do it together.

Chapter 17

MARGARET

There is no doubt in my mind that New Haven saved Lilo's life. From the moment I stepped onto the campus, I witnessed the high degree of professionalism, respect, and passion the entire staff had for the kids. They did not just care about the students but also about their families. To help the students heal, the families had to find healing as well.

Lilo was assigned to the Saratoga Springs campus and arrived on July 22, 2019. I knew from my virtual tour that the campus was like no other I had previously experienced. No pictures can do this campus justice. New Haven is not the least bit secluded but surrounded by other schools, retail, restaurants, and residential neighborhoods. Despite its location within the community, there are wide-open spaces with horses and stables. Although some team homes are connected, they are separate living units, and each is named for inspiring and influential historical women. I was amazed at how much it truly felt like a home away from home. The school has its own building, and just outside the main entrance is the family alumni wall. When a student is transitioning from New Haven, the family designs and paints a tile together to be placed on this wall. I walked by this wall too many times to count during my visits. And I did not fully understand the significance of its meaning until we presented our tile on the day of Lilo's transition.

As much as I loved New Haven from the start, not every day was perfect. There was a tremendous amount of work that was required of the student and the family. Lilo and I worked through the program simultaneously. We had weekly virtual family sessions in addition to

Lilo's individual and group therapy. I also attended and participated in parent weekends.

In fact, I visited New Haven for the very first time during a parents' weekend in September. Lilo was hoping to convince me to bring them home. I felt that we were already making progress, so my intention was to absolutely complete the program. Lilo was livid; therefore, they did everything they could that weekend to pull me out of my comfort zone and challenge me at every turn. Lilo volunteered the two of us for every therapeutic activity. This forced me to be my most vulnerable in front of all the other parents and students. On more than one occasion, Lilo left the room when they did not like my answer to a difficult question regarding our relationship. I helped lead a couple of trust activities even when my own child refused to participate. I worked extraordinarily hard that weekend, but I will forever be grateful for the lessons learned.

One of the greatest blessings at New Haven was Lilo's therapist, Melanie. I had met her during my virtual tour. I cannot articulate why or how, but I just knew she would be the perfect fit for our family. Her genuineness and subtle confidence made me certain that she and Lilo would have no problem establishing a connection. During the first few weeks when Lilo and Melanie connected with me virtually for our family sessions, I could see the ease in which Lilo communicated in Melanie's presence. I understood the comfort and the safety Melanie provided Lilo because I felt it the first time we met in person during parents' weekend. Melanie guided and supported us both during all three days. It was never easy to leave Lilo after a visit, but Lilo was willing to stay and continue our work with Melanie's help.

I returned just a few weeks later in October for New Haven's camping trip to Moab. Although the nights were quite cold, the days at Arches National Park were breathtaking. The activities and traditions celebrated there are some of my most special memories of Lilo's time in Utah.

I found the staff's ability to collaborate as a team one of New Haven's most impressive practices. The therapists and residential directors met together on a weekly basis to discuss and formulate the best strategies for supporting each individual student. I was comforted knowing that Lilo had a team of professionals who were working together to coordinate the best possible care for them.

New Haven was also instrumental in helping to develop Lilo's latent talent in writing poetry. They made it possible for Lilo to participate in poetry slams at Brigham Young University. They encouraged Lilo's creativity and assisted with the murder-mystery dinners Lilo put together. The school had sports teams and agreed to Lilo's idea of a dance team. New Haven fostered the interests of all the students. The students went to New Haven's athletic events, restaurants, movies, and plays. Some students even had part-time jobs. The kids were very much a part of the community, and Lilo was allowed the freedom to find themself.

As our work continued at New Haven, my maternal guilt kicked in about my initial choice to send Lilo to Missouri. We had a very honest conversation, and I admitted that I was aware of New Haven in 2017, when I first made the difficult decision to send them to residential. I have never forgotten Lilo's response to me. They immediately confessed that they would never have been ready for New Haven a few years earlier. They acknowledged that their experience in Missouri was necessary to mature and understand the work and commitment required to make changes at New Haven. Otherwise, Utah would have just been a repeat performance of Missouri. In a matter of minutes, Lilo's words allowed me to let go of my self-doubt about past decisions I was forced to make. I was tremendously comforted knowing that their past struggles led to their current breakthrough.

When the pandemic hit, the plans that Melanie, Lilo, and I had made for them to start interviewing for a job and to complete all behind-the-wheel requirements to acquire their driver's license came to a sudden halt. It was difficult to no longer travel back and forth to Utah. But it was most difficult to be separated from Lilo on their eighteenth birthday in May of 2020; however, missing their birthday proved to be my proudest moment. Lilo was discharged from New Haven on their birthday because I had signed them in while they were still a minor. Yet Lilo's first decision as a legal adult was to turn around and sign themself back into New Haven. Lilo was just a few short weeks away from high-school graduation in June.

They then would have one additional month before successfully completing the program at New Haven.

Sarah, Brooke, and I traveled to Utah for Lilo's high-school graduation on June 19, 2020. All festivities were held outside, so after thorough COVID-19 testing, the graduates' families could attend graduation. I still have no idea how Lilo managed to graduate from high school on time after years of hospitalizations and residential placements. They also graduated with honors in addition to receiving English and leadership awards.

Sarah and Brooke celebrating Lilo's high-school graduation—June 19, 2020

It was during this trip when the four of us painted our family tile to be placed on the wall at New Haven. We had no trouble at all deciding exactly what we would paint. During Lilo's years of various placements around the country, Priscilla remained in constant contact with them. She consistently sent cards and letters of encouragement to Lilo. There was one card from Priscilla that was especially meaningful. On the front was a dragonfly, and the card contained an explanation as to its meaning and significance. The dragonfly is considered to symbolize *change, transformation, adaptability,* and *self-realization.* The *change* that is often referred to has its source in mental and emotional maturity and understanding the deeper meaning of life. Lilo shared this card with us. Without any discussion, our family naturally adopted the dragonfly as another family symbol, in addition to the three stars representing our three children.

That afternoon, as we all painted a dragonfly and three stars onto our tile, Lilo began to cry when thinking about us leaving Utah without them in just a couple days. Lilo had roughly four more weeks until they completed the program and transitioned home. Lilo insisted they return home with us immediately and not complete the program. The two of us went outside to get a breath of fresh air. We sat down on an enormous rock, and Lilo cried in my arms. With tears streaming as I promised to return in July to bring them home permanently, not one, but two dragonflies flew right within reach of both of us. We were stunned into silence yet both felt instantly at peace. Lilo and I came to the same conclusion: Jeff and Priscilla were both with us, and we needed to finish this program together so that we could move forward without any regret.

I returned to Utah for Lilo's transition ceremony on July, 14, 2020. Priscilla, Sarah, and Brooke were able to join us virtually. I have no words to describe my emotions on that day. Lilo had been hospitalized for the very first time four years and three months before this transition. I was bringing them home permanently during the start of a pandemic, and I was not terrified. Sarah's college commencement had been canceled, but we were hopeful that her job would begin on schedule in September. The future was definitely uncertain. I suddenly would have all three kids under one roof, but I was not scared because I knew Lilo was ready.

I found our silver lining during the pandemic. *The world slowed down so that Lilo could reintegrate back into it.* I was given the opportunity to teach them to drive when no one was on the road. They found a part-time job very close to our home. Lilo was able to catch up on all life's practical lessons that they had missed while away from home for so many years.

Margaret and Lilo together during the transition ceremony at New Haven—July 14, 2020

I am relieved to share that New Haven was our last experience with residential treatment centers. I cannot articulate how grateful I am to have found them. The most difficult part of leaving New Haven was saying goodbye to Melanie, but we are still in touch with many people we met while there. New Haven saved my child's life, and the state of Utah will always have a very special place in my heart.

EPILOGUE

As I reflect on Lilo's mental health journey and my role within it, I am profoundly grateful for the relationship we have today. We have both come to a place of peace and acceptance surrounding the events we experienced together.

As I look back, many of our struggles are overwhelming to recall. Often I was overwhelmed by the decisions I was forced to make, the speed in which I had to make them, and the lack of resources available for struggling adolescents. I am also in awe of the lessons I learned and the many extraordinary people who have come into our lives as a result of this journey.

I sincerely believe that the lessons Lilo has taught me have led to our healing. As I stated at the beginning of this book, Lilo will forever be the greatest teacher in my life. They showed me that there is no one way or right way to view the world. They taught me that just because one's path and choices are different from my own, they are by no means wrong or less significant. Lilo urged me to listen more and to literally stop talking. As a parent, I wanted to fix their pain and pull them out of the darkness. Lilo did not need me to fix them; Lilo needed me to hear them.

Lilo also slowed me down so I could *be present* in the moment. I have always rushed through life in order to move on to the next thing. I can now actually stop and smell the roses and enjoy all life's small moments with my children. Lilo and I continue to have typical disagreements, as any mother and child do, but it's no longer catastrophic to our relationship. We are now at peace with who we are, and have learned to navigate the nuances of our relationship. Every day is not perfect, but we work hard to regulate our tone and actively listen to each other. Lilo is also well versed in using various coping strategies to manage their emotions. The ups and downs are no longer as extreme, so our relationship is much more balanced.

To those who may be desperately trying to guide an adolescent struggling with mental health, do not give up, because there is always hope. Advocate as loudly as possible and as often as is necessary. Meet with counselors and school officials regarding available services and accommodations. As difficult as it may be, do not be afraid to share your struggles with others. It is when we have the courage to air our dirty laundry that others will share theirs as well. You never know who may be helpful in finding the right therapist, support group, or program. I found that persistence proved to be invaluable in obtaining the help Lilo needed. I spent two years battling my insurance company and filing appeals to receive my child's entitled benefits. I called them every thirty days and told and retold my story to every representative who answered the phone. Whenever I was not heard and my needs not met, I hung up, called them back, and stated my case all over again to the next representative. It was incredibly frustrating, and I spent hours on hold until eventually I found that one person who was willing and patient enough to guide me through the process. I was emotionally exhausted and lived in tremendous fear for several years. But this taught me how vital self-care is during times of stress. When your child is dealing with trauma, as parents, it is only natural that their trauma becomes ours—and it takes unimaginable strength to ask and then receive professional help.

With loss come blessings. Our greatest blessing, without a moment of hesitation, is Priscilla Brinkman, who provided the professional help we desperately needed. When we first met, I had no idea the incredible impact she would have on me and my family. Her ability and willingness to think outside the box while treating Lilo and then me not only helped to save my child's life but also enabled me to keep my family intact. She read, researched, networked, and attended seminars to learn more about treatment strategies that could potentially help Lilo. Priscilla never allowed me to be or feel alone. She walked right beside me throughout our entire journey, and together we created the best team possible to support Lilo upon their return home. I will never find the right words—or enough words—to express the gratitude I feel or to articulate what a truly special member of our family she has become.

I experienced one of the most beautiful moments of the writing process while sitting outside on my patio. I was writing one of the most difficult chapters of this book and reliving the darkest and most terrorizing time of my life. I found that I had to keep reminding myself that Lilo is no longer in that devastatingly dark place. As I was writing, my cell phone began to ring. I picked up the phone, and Lilo enthusiastically shared that they had just been awarded a scholarship at their community college. It was at this very moment that I became acutely aware of just how far we have come. The child that once definitively stated that they would never reach their eighteenth birthday has enrolled in community college. Lilo is living independently and maintaining a job as they go to school.

I could not be more proud of my amazing child, and I know Jeff would be also. Lilo is a remarkable young adult. They are authentically and unapologetically themself—incredibly talented, bright, and one of the most loving human beings I have ever known. I could not love and adore them more than I do for exactly who they are. Lilo was placed into Jeff's and my arms for a very special reason. I am a much more accepting, empathetic, and content mother, daughter, sister, and friend because of the lessons I learned from my child. We have survived incredible darkness and found the light. We have learned to ***let go*** of the trauma, the fear, the guilt, and the resentment so that we can carry Jeff with us in our hearts and ***love forever.***

—Margaret

Dear reader,

You may not know me, but now you know my story. I may not know you, but I do know that you are loved and worth fighting for. You may or may not believe these words, but I *believe* in you. I believe that you are here for a reason and that you also read this book for a reason.

We are so quick to judge ourselves and others based on superficial labels, past mistakes, and past identities, but I don't believe that is all a person is. I know this because I have watched my mother grow and transform through her struggles. When my father died, my mother went from the loving wife to the grieving widow overnight. She is a survivor. But to be a survivor, you have to be so much more.

She got out of bed on days when she felt so utterly alone. She helped dress her three children for school until they were old enough to do it themselves. She cooked us meals, barely slept, and created a scholarship in my father's name after his passing. She dealt with losing her hair behind closed doors, helped prepare us for high school and college, and got us ready to go out into the world without her. She was the knot that held our family together when we all felt broken. On top of all that, she dealt with keeping me alive every day. She was under extreme stress from friends and family telling her what she should do, what she should say, and how she should act to deal with everything the universe was throwing at her. My mother had the weight of the world on her shoulders, and she still fought.

My mother isn't just a survivor; she's a fighter. She's someone who will look in the mirror each day and find ways to better herself by staying healthy, strengthening her friendships, and laughing so hard with her children that we all cry. She takes time to actively learn about my mental health and what it means to have a child who is a part of the LGBTQIA+ community, instead of turning me away because I'm not the "daughter" she wanted. My mother has given me an ear to listen and a shoulder to cry on.

My mother is willing to do whatever it takes for the people she loves the most. She puts love out into the world every day with her radiant smile. She always said my dad had the biggest smile in the room, but that's only because she couldn't see how big her own smile is and that he was probably glowing because he loved seeing her happy.

I have also been labeled a survivor, crazy, suicidal, and the kid with the dead dad. But that's not who I am. Those are labels based on what I've been through. I learned to survive after being in and out of residential facilities for most of my teenage years. When I was released into the world, I didn't know how to write a check, drive a car, or do laundry. I'd never experienced what most teenagers do, and yet I learned. I learned how to do simple things like open a bank account, legally change my name, live on my own, and hold down a job. I didn't know how to come out and be open about my sexuality, but I still learned. And not long after I graduated from New Haven, I made a new friend who saw how comfortable I was in my skin, and she trusted me to be the first person she came out to. There's power in owning your identity, even when you have to start over completely.

Today, I am resilient. I am no longer the scared child wanting to hurt myself to escape. Instead, I am a powerful human being. I am a writer, an author, and a poet. I am a dancer, a dreamer, an overthinker, and a creator. I am a proud transmasculine-nonbinary person, a drag artist, and someone who accepts people for who they are. I am strong, and I am a fighter. I don't give up even when death sometimes feels like the right choice in the moment. I am a learner and a teacher. I like to feel my emotions deeply. I like understanding where our feelings originate and learning how to heal our souls. I like to mold words to beautiful people through poetry to help them understand what I see in them. I am a caretaker for my dog, Tyson. I am a friend and sibling to Sarah, Brooke, and my half-siblings. I believe family doesn't mean you are blood related. I want to spend my life laughing, traveling, watching sunsets, and being adventurous, all while radiating love. I want to dance with my extended family at wedding receptions, as we all find love eventually. I want to learn about who people truly are inside. Most importantly, I want to love openly and willingly as I meet new souls along this journey.

I am beyond grateful to have the family who raised me and to now know my birth family. My birth father was killed about a year after I located him. I believe that was a sign that I never "needed" a dad to be normal. His death brought me closer to my birth sister, who I eventually met in person. Family isn't about blood; it's about who will choose to love you and accept you at your best and worst. I am lucky to move forward in life with two families who mean the world to me.

But just because I move forward doesn't mean I forget the pain. We need our pain. Without that deep pain, we won't ever be able to feel the immense happiness, excitement, or deepest joys of life. Life isn't about "finding happiness" and just enjoying life. That's not realistic. Happiness passes just like any other feeling, so it can never be your final destination. The destination is feeling everything to the fullest and experiencing life with love in your heart. That's our purpose: to live to the fullest. Live with pain, grief, joy, excitement, anxiety, depression, sadness, happiness, but most of all, *love*.

If you have ever questioned whether you are good enough, if you're enough, or if all this pain is worth it, take a look in the mirror. Don't judge your body, your past mistakes, or the traumas you've been through. Look in the mirror a little more closely. Look yourself in the eye and really see yourself. Take it all in. See how much you have been through—your struggles and your triumphs. See what this universe has chosen to put you through on your journey. See yourself in totality—whether you feel confident in who you are or your reflection brings tears to your eyes. You are here to live, you lovely human being, and I promise you that you deserve to live. I love you for you, and one day, if you aren't there yet, you will start to understand why.

As you close these pages, I hope you feel less alone. I hope you have found ways to help yourself grieve if you have lost. If you are a parent trying to keep your child alive or a friend of someone suicidal, I hope you have learned to stay by their side and to listen more instead of talking. If you are struggling to get out of bed, I hope you have found some hope that you might be able to laugh and smile authentically again. If you are scared to cry and be vulnerable, I hope you have found a new understanding that feeling your emotions is one of the strongest things you can do. If you are a therapist, I hope you know you are valued, loved, and supported every bit as much as your clients.

If you are thinking about taking those pills, cutting, jumping, etc., I sincerely hope you trust me when I say it's not your time. I don't have to know you to understand that your feelings, as intense as they feel in those moments, do pass. You won't feel this way forever. Yes, they might come back again, and that's exactly why I hope you let yourself feel before letting them pass. Without them, happiness doesn't feel as great. I hope you live another day, and I hope you find love in this life, because you deserve love.

Thank you for diving into my world and my mind. As Brooke said years ago, "Sometimes you have to *let go*, in order to *love forever*." Let go of what's holding you back from living your life to the fullest. As you embrace each new tomorrow, keep yourself open to love—love for yourself, love for others, and love in each and every moment.

With love,
Lilo Baurer

★★★

Dear Dad,

I know you can't be here to witness the amount of growth we have all made as a family, but I believe you still know. As the days go by, it becomes harder to remember your voice, your smile, and the smell of your cologne. But I still feel you. I know you're with me in the waves, the horizon, and each sunrise and sunset. That's how I know it's okay to move forward with my life without you. I know you wanted us to all be who we are happily and authentically. I learned to live like that because of you. I love you always.

Love,
Lilo

LILO BAURER - MENTAL HEALTH TIMELINE

3/24/2016 – 4/06/2016 **FIRST PHP** 3/22/2016 Self-injury 3/23/2016 Intake	9/05/2016 **PSYCHOLOGICAL EVALUATION** “Major Depressive Disorder” “Unspecified Anxiety Disorder”	9/13/2016 – 9/30/2016 **PHP** 2nd admission Same location 9/12/2016 Self-injured at high school
1/25/2017 **504 ELIGIBILITY MEETING** Signed document received	6/07/2017 **PICKED UP BY LOCAL POLICE TICKET-CURFEW VIOLATION (1:06 AM)**	6/07/2017 **LILO REFUSES TREATMENT POLICE ESCORT FROM HOME TO ER**
8/17/2017 (Half Day) **ENROLL SUBURBAN CATHOLIC** **HIGH SCHOOL** 8/21/2017 1st full day of school “Hail Mary”	8/23/2017 – 8/30/2017 **INPATIENT** New Location 8/23/2017 Self-injured in restroom at school	9/01/2017 – 12/17/2018 **RESIDENTIAL** Lux Residential Treatment Center PROFESSIONAL TRANSPORT **LAUNCH** (4/09/2018–4/12/2018) **Lilo officially adopts Tyson**
2/23/2019 – 3/19/2019 **INPATIENT** Another New Location 3/7/2019 Planned discharge Patient advocate forces 2nd opinion 2/22/2019 Swallowed 50 low-dose aspirin	2/27/2019 **HIRE EDUCATIONAL CONSULTANT** Assist with IEP (Individualized Education Plan) Determine next steps	3/08/2019 **FORMAL REQUEST FOR AN INITIAL CASE STUDY EVALU-ATION TO DETERMINE IEP ELIGIBILITY**
7/22/2019 **IEP ELIGIBILITY MEETING**	7/22/2019 – 7/14/2020 **RESIDENTIAL** New Haven - Saratoga Springs, Utah PROFESSIONAL TRANSPORT **GRADUATION** – 6/19/2020 **TRANSITION HOME** – 7/14/2020	

Week of 10/10/2016
REQUEST 504 PLAN
(Determine accommodations)
10/10/2016
School personnel request a 4-week review period

12/13/2016 – 12/16/2016
INPATIENT
1st admission
Suburban Hospital
12/12/2016
Self-injury, cutting, string around neck

12/19/2016 – 1/11/2017
PHP
3rd admission
Same location

6/08/2017 – 6/16/2017
INPATIENT
2nd admission
Same hospital

6/16/2017 – 7/30/2017
RESIDENTIAL
Concordia Health
Indiana
TRANSPORTED BY CONCORDIA

8/08/2017 – 8/22/2017
DBT GROUP THERAPY
(Dialectical Behavior Therapy)
Twice weekly

9/17/2018
ENROLL FUSION ACADEMY & LEARNING CENTER
Oak Brook, IL
Attends during home visits and holidays until Lux transition; 2nd semester junior year begins 1/07/2019

12/19/2018 – 1/12/2019
INPATIENT
Brookview
12/18/2018
(24 hours after Lux transition)
ER–severe cutting, nicked artery

1/15/2018 – 2/08/2019
PHP
New suburban location

3/19/2019 – 4/09/2019
RESIDENTIAL
Concordia Health
Indiana
TRANSPORTED BY CONCORDIA
Used as "safe place" while waited for assessment program opening

4/09/2019 – 7/22/2019
RESIDENTIAL DIAGNOSTIC ASSESSMENT PROGRAM
PROFESSIONAL TRANSPORT
Average stay 30–45 days

5/08/2019
ENGAGE LEGAL COUNSEL
Represent Lilo's best interests

ACKNOWLEDGMENTS

To our family for their unconditional love and endless support.

To Priscilla, we would not be here without you.

To Margaret's "forever" dance moms for their love, guidance, non-judgment, and listening ears while sharing a bottle of wine.

To Suzy for always believing.

Last but certainly not least, to our team at Pithy Wordsmithery, most especially Amelia Forczak, Deanna Novak, Brian Walls, Devon Pine, and Chet Turnbeaugh.

ABOUT THE AUTHORS

Margaret Baurer is an advocate for parents and guardians seeking resources and standing up for change for their children. She is a mother of three children and currently lives in Illinois. Margaret enjoys traveling and reading and is a wine enthusiast.

Lilo Baurer is a champion for teens and young adults facing the troubled-teen industry, including mental health challenges. Lilo is currently a student pursuing a career as a licensed therapist. They are an avid writer, poet, and drag artist in Iowa, where they love to perform and express their gender identity. Lilo is an advocate for authenticity and self-expression when it comes to being a member of the LGBTQIA+ community.

To contact the authors: hello@hopewardhealing.com,
www.hopewardhealing.com

www.ingramcontent.com/pod-product-compliance
Lightning Source LLC
LaVergne TN
LVHW100315210926
848480LV00003B/1125